When It's Your Turn

Grown Children Caring for Aging Parents

Susan Shelly

B A
& N
B O
N E

Dedication

This book is dedicated to my mother, Kathryn E. Shelly, who, along with Dad, raised four caring children.

ISBN 0-7607-2699-x

Text design by Lundquist Design, New York

Printed and bound in the United States of America

02 03 04 05 MP 9 8 7 6 5 4 3 2 1

Introduction

You've raised, or are raising, your children. You have a home, a career, and plans for your future. You're at the point where you're considering buying that little place at the beach, or even thinking about retiring in a few years.

All of a sudden, everything changes. You get a call one night that your mother has fallen and is admitted to the hospital with a broken hip. Or, your father suffers a stroke and enters a nursing care facility for rehabilitation. A parent is diagnosed with cancer, or has a heart attack. The doctor tells you that she suspects Alzheimer's disease. Without warning, your life is turned inside out as you struggle to keep up with your own responsibilities, and, at the same time, help to care for Mom or Dad.

More and more baby boomers are caring for aging parents, and making major changes in their own lives as a result. Our parents are living longer, and many of us will be challenged to step up and take our turns as caregivers.

The purpose of this book is to provide useful information that will make caring for aging parents easier. You'll learn about some of the physical, mental, and emotional aspects of aging. You'll learn a great deal about helping your parents manage their finances. You'll learn about long-term health insurance, assisted living and nursing homes, wills and trusts, power of attorney, Medicare and Medicaid, and issues of death and dying. You'll also learn about taking care of yourself, and what is, or isn't feasible for you to do.

Stepping up to take your turn and care for aging parents is difficult, but having reliable information can help to make the task easier.

Acknowledgments

I would like to thank the many people who provided time, information, resources, and encouragement for this book. I also thank the editorial group—Heather Russell-Revesz, Kristin Shea, Mike Ferrari, and Rick Campbell.

And, many thanks to Bert Holtje and Gene Brissie of James Peter Associates. They are constant and dependable sources of encouragement, wisdom, and humor. Thanks also to Sarah Young Fisher, for her technical assistance.

Special appreciation goes to my sister-in-law, Julia Jorgensen Shelly, who was willing to share her memories—both happy and painful—of the years she cared for her elderly parents in her home. And, to my brother, James N. Shelly, Jr., for supporting Julia in her loving task.

Appreciation, also, to my best friend forever, Joan Zellers Morse, who meets the demands of the sandwich generation with grace and humor. And, to Marge Gibbons, for sharing her knowledge and expertise about matters relating to the elderly.

I could not complete these acknowledgments without remembering my wonderful grandmother, Ethel Klaus. At 103, "Granny" adds an extra and wonderful layer to our family's sandwich, and continues to inspire all of us.

My life has been richly and abundantly blessed with caring—both given and received. I truly hope that yours will be the same.

Table of Contents

Chapter One

Full Circle—Grown Children Caring for Aging Parents

Aging is an inevitable, and, when you consider the alternative, a desirable fact of life. Living into old age—the 80s and 90s—is become increasingly common. And, while it's nice to think that Mom and Dad will be around to see their grandchildren grow up, it also means that some of the burden associated with their aging probably will fall onto you.

The National Family Caregivers Association (NFCA), based in Kensington, Maryland, estimates that there are 25 million family caregivers in the United States. Nearly a quarter of these caregivers are watching over aging parents, while other are caring for grandparents, aunts, uncles, and other relatives. These caregivers of provide about two-thirds of all home care services. The NFCA estimates the value of these services at $300 billion a year.

Helping to care for aging parents or other relatives or friends can involve many different tasks and responsibilities. Chances are that when you accept the role of caregiver, you won't have a full understanding of what your responsibilities will entail until you've been at the job for a while. And, as your parents get older, more infirm, or just more dependent on you, those responsibilities are likely to increase.

In this chapter, we'll look at some implications of aging, and some of the common areas in which elderly people need assistance. We'll also discuss different aspects of wellness, and how to gauge the wellness—or lack of wellness—of an elderly person. While the focus of this book is caring for aging parents, with most of the information addressed to that issue, the contents certainly can apply to other relatives, neighbors, or friends, as well.

Accepting Your Role as Caregiver

Some people fall easily into the role of caregiver, while others find it does not come as naturally. The extent to which you'll be able to be your parent's caregiver depends on many factors, and it's important for you to fully and frankly assess your situation—and that of your parent—so you can make an honest, informed decision about what will work, and what won't.

Most of us love our parents deeply, and we want what's best for them. We want to help them as much as possible, and make their later years as pleasant and fulfilling as possible. What's involved in doing that, however, varies greatly from family to family.

If your parents are reasonably self reliant and only need your help once a month to write checks and look over their bills, your role as caregiver will be fairly limited, and chances are you won't feel overburdened. On the other hand, if they're on the phone three times a day, asking you to do everything from taking out the trash to figuring out the status of their federal income tax, you're likely to feel a little overwhelmed, and probably a bit resentful.

It's extremely important that you don't try to do everything concerning your parents' care by yourself. You'll quickly burn out, and you, your parents, and the rest of your family will suffer because of it. If you have siblings, call a family conference and discuss the role that each member will play. As you no doubt have discovered a long time ago, family relationships can become frayed very quickly. It's important that everyone understands what's going on, and has the same expectations regarding the care of aging parents.

Many families unofficially "appoint" one person as the primary caregiver, without ever consulting the chosen one. It somehow becomes understood that good old Janie will take care of Mom and Dad, whether or not Janie actually agreed to accept the role. Needless to say, this is not an ideal situation. Janie will quickly figure out what's happened, and, understandably, become resentful. If you find yourself in Janie's position, be sure to bring the matter to the attention of your siblings right away.

A survey by the National Family Caregivers Association shows that of the 25 million family caregivers in the United States, 81 percent are female, 79 percent are married, and 70 percent are between the ages of 40 and 60. On a scary note, nearly half of all caregivers are thought to suffer from prolonged depression.

If you're an only child, or you agree to be your parents' primary caregiver, know that there is help available. You'll learn more about what's out there, and how to find it, later in this book.

Acting as a caretaker for aging parents—regardless of in what form or to what extent—is a demanding job that can further pull on your already busy schedule. It also, however, can be extremely rewarding, and a good chance for you to return some of the love and care that your parents have given you throughout your life.

What You Might Have to do to Help

Some people remain self-sufficient into their 80s or 90s, keeping up homes or apartments, continuing to drive, taking care of their financial matters, and taking responsibility for their own health. Those people are extremely fortunate. More often than not, by the time people reach their mid-to-late 70s, they need some sort of assistance. It might not be much, or it could be a major undertaking for caregivers.

Perhaps the upkeep on your parents' home has become too much for them, and you end up mowing grass, trimming hedges, or cleaning windows every weekend. Or, maybe they can no longer handle their financial matters as well as they used to, and you need to step in and help with paying bills and keeping records. They might be struggling with estate planning, or with finding a more manageable place to live, or with selling a home.

The manner in which you may need to help aging parents varies greatly, depending on physical health, mental capacity, and other factors. Many, many people, however, find that their parents need help in the following areas:

- Managing their personal finances
- Estate planning
- Making decisions about where to live
- Coping with medical problems

- Dealing with the complexities of the health care system
- Figuring out insurance claims, bills, and so forth

Chances are, that if you're called up to be a caregiver for an aging parent, your work will encompass at least one of these categories.

When Parents Can No Longer Cope on Their Own

Having to tell your parents you think they need some help can be extremely difficult, both for you and for them. It's painful for a parent to have to face the fact that his relationship with a child is changing, or to feel that he is no longer in charge. To many people, needing help is a sign of incompetence or failure.

Older men who are accustomed to taking care of everything themselves may have great difficulty adjusting to the idea of needing assistance. A man of your father's generation, who's likely to have spent most his life taking care of his wife, children, finances, home, and so forth, is likely to resist the notion that he can no longer do so.

Sometimes the need for help is obvious. An injury or serious illness occurs, and it's clear to everyone that your parent can't cope on her own. Often, however, signs of needing help are harder to detect. Older people can be masterful at hiding their need for help, either because they don't want to admit that they need it, or because they don't want to be a bother. And, because many family members live far apart from one another, the need for help isn't always quickly recognized.

If you live in Chicago and your folks are in Philadelphia, chances are that you don't spend a lot of time together. Their situation may change significantly between your visits, and you might not know that they need help with household chores, managing finances, or whatever, until the situation has become very serious. If you do live a distance from your older parents and worry about what may be happening, it's a good idea to try to find a contact person who lives near them. Perhaps there's a neighbor, or a minister, priest, or rabbi who would call you they notice any problems concerning your parents. This could alert you to early problems, and make you feel more comfortable about being away.

If both your parents are living, and they live together, one parent may express concerns to you about the other. Maybe Mom confides that she's terribly worried about Dad because he has frequent chest pain but refuses to see a doctor. Or, Dad might pull you aside to tell you that Mom's forgetfulness has gotten to the point where she can't keep track of her medications. If that happens, be sure to take the concerns seriously, and start thinking about how you might help. Your dad is likely to have remained quiet about his concerns for a long time for fear of being "disloyal" to your mom. By the time he finally talks to you about the problem, chances are it's quite serious. If you have brothers and sisters, remember to tell them about your concerns and get their input on how you might help your parents.

Sometimes, grown children are aware that their parents are having problems, but they choose to minimize or ignore them. They might brush off the problems as being a normal part of aging, or rationalize that everything must be fine because Mom hasn't called for two weeks. This can happen because the child is reluctant to confront the situation. He might be scared about how his parents' problems will affect his own family, or if he'll have time to help his folks and keep up with his demanding career. Maybe he recognizes and is upset by the fact that his parents are getting old.

The parent-child bond is unique, and it doesn't end on the day you move out of your parents' house, or when you get married, or when you have a child of your own. The bond is always there, and seeing the relationship between your parents and yourself change can be painful and difficult. To help your parents, however, you need to be able to look at their situation as objectively as possibly and be willing to be their advocate.

Knowing When It's Time to Step In

Ideally, you're able to talk frankly to your parents about whatever's going on in their lives, and they willingly tell you about any problems they're having. If they're having trouble handling their finances, it's great if you're able sit down with them, talk about the difficulty, and work with them to solve it.

Unfortunately, real life often isn't like that. Your dad might feel ashamed to tell you that he can't figure out the bills anymore, much less deal with his income taxes. It may be next to impossible for your mother to discuss with you the problems she's having with incontinence, much less ask you to buy her Depends.

Knowing when to step in and insist that your parents get some help is a difficult decision. You know that it's good for your parents to be as independent as possible, and limiting their independence by even offering help can be risky. They might be offended by your suggestion that they need help, or they may be worried that they're becoming a burden. When you step over the parent-child line, regardless of age or circumstances, you change your relationship with your parents, and that can be painful to you and to them.

There are circumstances, however, which make it necessary for you to act on behalf of your parents, whether or not they want you to. They include:

- When their safety is at stake. If your mother has burned the bottom of every pot she owns because she forgets to turn off the stove when she's finished cooking, or your father gets confused when he walks to the neighborhood store and can't find his way back home, there's no question that it's time to step in.
- One parent has become too much of a burden on the other. Maybe your mom would never admit it that caring for your dad has gotten to be too much for her. But, if she's staying up all night to make sure he doesn't wander out of the house during his nighttime ramblings, or she's become verbally or physically abusive toward him due to a mental condition, it's time to do something.
- Circumstances are clearly out of control. You try to call your folks and find out their phone has been disconnected because they didn't pay the bill. Or, you realize that they have allowed their bills to pile up. Maybe the electricity is going to be shut off. Or, you discover that they haven't been to the grocery store for three weeks because of the difficulty of going there and getting the groceries back home. These, and similar situations, are obvious signs that help is necessary.
- When the situation becomes too trying for the rest of the family. Maybe your mother doesn't think it's a big deal that she's fallen four times in the last six months, but you're worried sick that her next fall will be down the basement steps. Or, your sister flies across the country twice a month to cook dinners for your father's freezer because she knows that's the only way he'll eat decent meals. Independence is important, but, when it comes at a price that's too high for other family members, it's time to step in.

If you do need to step in and take control, at least temporarily, your parents might react in one of several ways. If they realize the situation has gotten out of hand or that it's too difficult for them, they may be grateful to have help. They may have been hoping someone would come to their aid, even if they were reluctant to ask for help. Or, they could resist your efforts to help. If that happens, you'll need to be firm and explain exactly why you feel that help for them is necessary. Either way, it's important that you act in a manner that will help them maintain their dignity.

Guarding Their Dignity

There are different ways to handle any situation, and dealing with your parents when you've decided it's necessary to step in and help them is no exception. Some people become angry and resentful when faced with the burden of caring for aging parents. Some become martyrs—doing what they are called upon to do. Some respond by treating their aging parents like children, moving in to do every little thing for them. None of these attitudes is productive.

The best way to respond when it's time to step in, is to do so in a matter-of-fact manner that protects your parents' dignity. They're your parents. They don't want to be treated like children. They don't want to be told what they have to do, or where they have to live, or what foods they have to eat. When it's time to step in, keep these tips in mind on how to help your parents maintain their pride and dignity.

- Consult with them about what you plan to do. If it's obvious that your parents can no longer handle their financial affairs, sit down and talk to them about it. Don't make arrangements to change the way they've always done things without talking with them first.
- Give them options. Would they rather that you come once a month to help with paying bills and keeping track of investments, or would they prefer to have their financial adviser or lawyer take care of it? Nobody likes to be told what to do, especially someone who has been living independently for a long time.
- Consider their feelings. Chances are that your father is somewhat humiliated that his phone service was shut down because he forgot to pay the bill for three months. Assure him that this problem occurs with other people, as well, and talk with him respectfully about how to deal with it.
- Don't treat them like children. Your parents remain your parents as long as they live. They don't want to be treated like children, and, although your roles may largely reverse, you should continue to acknowledge their parental status.

Every family has its own ideas and expectations about aging, relationships, independence, and other matters that affect children and parents. Hopefully, you and your parents have similar philosophies and attitudes concerning important life issues, and you understand and respect one another's viewpoints. No, you won't agree on every issue that arises, and you might find that it's sometimes necessary to insist on handling a situation in a particular way. Treating your aging parents with respect and dignity, however, will go a long way in making your changing relationship more comfortable and easier to deal with.

What is Aging?

We're all aging—every day. But, aging is more than simply getting older. Aging is coming face to face with major, and often unwanted, life changes. Retiring from a job you've had for years, moving from the house in which you've raised your family, losing a spouse, learning that you have early signs of Alzheimer's disease.

Think about what it must be like to lose a spouse after 30, 40, or 50 years of marriage. Or to leave a career that has provided you with a sense of identity and purpose for the past 30 or 40 years. Or to have to decide which half of your possessions you'll keep and which you'll need to sell before the move to a smaller, more manageable place. Or to start planning how you'll cope, and help others to cope, with the devastating disease you've just learned you have.

This isn't to say that aging is one long, sad series of bad news. Many people live happy, fulfilling lives well into old age. Aging does, however, carry with it some challenges.

Those of us who have lost a parent or other person close to us know how difficult it is to deal with that kind of loss. Still, our loss is tempered by the comforting presence of our own families, busy lives, daily routines, friends, careers, and so forth. An elderly person who loses a spouse often must deal with the loss of her life as she knows it. She loses not only her husband, but her sense of identity, her daily routine, and her sense of her place in the world. Effectively, she's been cut adrift from the life she knew, and is forced to make a new one.

Aging brings about physical, mental, and emotional changes. Let's take a look at how your parents—and you—might deal with these age-related changes as they occur.

Dealing with Physical Changes

No doubt, you've seen some physical changes of your own, and you probably don't even fall into the categories of "aging" or "elderly." Maybe you hair is a bit thinner or grayer than it used to be, your waistline somewhat expanded, and those lines around your eyes a bit more noticeable. Maybe you've noticed that it's harder to climb the stairs than it used to be, and your doctor is keeping an eye on your blood pressure and cholesterol levels.

As we get older, we encounter many physical changes. Organs such as the lungs, kidneys, and heart work less efficiently than they used to. Bones become less dense and more brittle. Skin becomes less elastic and starts to sag. The senses, particularly sight and hearing, often become impaired. Hair changes in color and texture. These changes don't mean that elderly people should expect to be sick, or that their body systems will inevitably break down. Everyone, however, should be aware of the changes that normally occur with aging, and be prepared to deal with them as they do.

The American Medical Association reports that, between the ages of 30 and 74, the efficiency of the heart decreases by about 30 percent, and that of the lungs by about 40 percent. The liver becomes 10 percent less efficient, and the kidneys about 40 percent less efficient.

Lifestyle changes may be necessary to accommodate physical changes. Perhaps your elderly parent can no longer manage in a house with several sets of stairs. Or, assistive devices may be necessary in order for her to see or hear. How your aging parents might deal with physical changes depends on several factors. If they're generally healthy and active, normal physical changes might mean nothing more drastic than changing their weekly tennis match from singles to doubles, or using a pull cart instead of carrying their clubs on the golf course. If they're not in overall good health, physical changes may have a more profound effect.

You can help them deal with physical changes by encouraging them to remain active and to exercise for as long as possible, to eat nutritious, balanced meals, to see a doctor regularly, and to avoid unhealthy practices such as smoking or excessive alcohol consumption.

Dealing With Mental Changes

Changes also occur to the brain as we age. It becomes smaller and lighter, and brain cells die at a faster rate than when we're younger. Some loss of memory—especially short term memory—is common due to these changes. And, your aging parent might seem a bit slower mentally. Maybe it takes your father longer to add up his monthly bills than it used to, or your mother has a difficult time calculating what the items on her grocery list will cost.

These changes don't mean that your parent has lost intelligence, or has Alzheimer's disease or another form of dementia. Mental changes are common in aging persons, and you should reassure Mom that not being able to remember the names of every person in her exercise class does not mean that she's become senile.

The fear of becoming mentally disabled is great among elderly people, and not something that should be taken lightly. A physician should be consulted about any signs of serious mental confusion or other mental disorders, since an underlying disorder can cause symptoms that mimic dementia.

Dealing With Lifestyle Changes

Most elderly persons are forced to make some lifestyle changes. Those who are lucky get away with hiring someone to take care of the yard instead of doing it themselves, or taking the train to visit a relative instead of driving.

Many people, however, must make more drastic changes, such as leaving their homes, giving up their cars, or learning to live without their spouses. Those who haven't planned financially, or never had the opportunity to make or save much money, might be forced to scale back their lifestyles due to financial concerns.

You can help parents with lifestyle changes by being supportive and understanding, and allowing them to make as many of their own decisions as possible. Don't minimize the importance of any of these types of changes, regardless of how unimportant or insignificant they might seem to you. While it may seem trivial to you that your mother is no longer able to see well enough to thread the needle of her sewing machine, that loss to her could signify the beginning of not being able to do for herself, which could be extremely distressing to her. You might make jokes about how the roadways are safer because your dad turned in his driver's license, while to him no longer being able to drive is a traumatic loss. Be sensitive to what lifestyle changes mean to them.

Emotional Changes Might be the Hardest of All

When our parents are sick, we can take them to see a doctor. If Dad's hearing fails, we can help him to get a hearing aid. If Mom can no longer handle the steps in her house, we can help her to find a first-floor condo or apartment.

Emotional changes, however, are more difficult to recognize and to deal with. You expect your mother to grieve after your father dies, but is it normal for her to break into tears every time she tries to talk about him? And, why does your father get so angry whenever you ask him about his plans to sell the family home and move into a smaller place? Why is you mother suddenly so fearful about leaving the house?

We all deal with emotional ups and downs throughout our lives, but these changes may become exaggerated in elderly persons. Your mother may experience feelings of hopelessness after your father dies. Your father might retire and feel useless and burdensome. Understanding how they feel, and being willing to talk with your parents about these kinds of issues can be extremely helpful, both to them and to you. If you think they'd be receptive, you might arrange for them to meet with a counselor. Or, have them talk to their minister, priest, or rabbi. If emotional changes seem very severe and lasting, try to arrange for your parent to have an evaluation with a doctor. Depression is common in older people, or what seems to be an emotional problem could actually be caused by a physical problem.

Men who are 65 or older have the highest suicide rate of any age group in the country, with those 85 and older being especially at risk. People who are 65-plus make up only about 13 percent of the U.S. population, but they (mostly men) account for 20 percent of all suicides.

Aging, and all that comes with it, is rarely easy. There are problems, and losses, and changes that nobody asks for. As children of aging parents, we can only do our best to help make their aging as healthy and happy as possible.

What is Wellness—Physical, Mental and Financial?

Although you might think it seems odd to discuss physical, mental and financial wellness together, it probably makes more sense than you think.

Health and finances are two of the greatest areas of concern to elderly persons, and, in many ways, they're closely linked. What older person hasn't wondered whether he or she will have enough money to live comfortably for the rest of his or her life, or worried there will be any money left to pass on to children and grandchildren? What about the expenses involved with in-home health care or a nursing home? Will he be able to afford all the necessary prescription medicines?

Being financially healthy doesn't guarantee that an older person will remain physically and/or mentally healthy. It does, however, alleviate a lot of anxiety concerning the cost of health care, nursing care, and other matters. Wellness—physical, mental, and financial—is a sense of having control. Wellness doesn't mean a complete lack of problems, but it implies that there's a means of dealing with problems that do occur.

Physical and Mental Wellness

We already mentioned some of the physical and mental changes that occur as people age, and some of the problems that occur as results of those changes. Sight and hearing diminish, along with the efficiency of major organs. Bones thin and break more easily as a result. Brain cells die off. Older people, however, can experience these changes and still maintain a sense of physical wellness.

Your mother, as nearly everyone else her age, has probably experienced some loss of bone density, but that doesn't mean that she isn't well. Your father may not hear as well as he used to, and maybe he's gotten a little bit forgetful, but you don't consider him to be sick because of those conditions. These and similar issues might be problems, but they are problems that you can deal with.

Some problems, however, are more serious and threatening to the wellness of your parent. Mild arthritis that makes it a little hard to get out of bed in the morning is one issue, but crippling, disfiguring arthritis is quite a different one. A bit of forgetfulness is very different than dementia that robs a person of her memory, the people she loves, and the very person she used to be. We all know about heart disease and cancer, both major causes of death, but we might not be as much aware of conditions such as macular degeneration, diabetes, or anxiety disorders.

Recognizing serious threats to physical wellness is important, because it means a problem can be treated early, with better chance for recovery. Some common physical conditions associated with aging include those listed below. Remember, though, that although these conditions are common, they're not a normal part of aging, like gray hair or bifocals. Symptoms of these conditions should never be ignored.

- **Diabetes.** This is a serious disease that affects 15.7 million Americans, according to the American Diabetes Center. Although some people think of diabetes as a childhood disease, Type 2 diabetes, or adult-onset diabetes, affects nearly one in every 12 people age 65 or over. A big problem with this type of diabetes is that it often goes undetected and untreated. Symptoms include fatigue, weight loss, blurred vision, extreme hunger or thirst, and itchy skin. Women are more at risk than men, and those who are overweight and inactive have increased chances of getting diabetes.
- **Eye Problems.** Everyone who lives long enough will eventually develop presbyopia, which is the loss of ability to focus up close, and is derived from a Latin word that translates literally into "old eyes." By the time we hit 40 or so, many of us need glasses or contacts in order to see what we used to see without them. But, while conditions such as myopia (nearsightedness) and hyperopia (farsightedness) are common and correctable, other eye conditions are far more worrisome. Cataracts, glaucoma, and macular degeneration are the three big problems that affect many older eyes, and all can cause devastating loss of sight if left untreated. Impaired distance vision, poor night vision, blurred vision, the need to change eyeglass prescriptions frequently, double vision in one eye, and appearance of a halo around lights are possible symptoms. Glaucoma is particularly dangerous because it has not obvious symptoms. Macular degeneration is an extremely serious disease, for which there is no cure at this time. Symptoms vary, but may include a wavy appearance to straight surfaces, trouble adjusting from sunshine to dim lighting, and trouble reading because letters and words appear distorted. Regular eye exams are extremely important for older people.
- **Incontinence.** Urinary incontinence is very common in older people, especially women. It's not, however, a normal part of aging, and often can be corrected or the condition improved. There are three major types of incontinence: stress, overflow, and urge. Each has a different cause. Many people are reluctant to discuss the problem of incontinence, even with their doctors. It's serious because it can cause people to become isolated. Many people choose to stay at home, rather than risk having an "accident" in public. If you suspect an aging parent may be having a problem with incontinence, urge her to discuss the matter with her physician.

- **Osteoporosis.** Osteoporosis, or porous bones, is a big problem, especially among aging women. Men get it too, but not nearly as often as women, because women typically experience more loss of bone mass than men. Many people suffer from osteoporosis and never know it, until they break a bone. Calcium supplements can help to maintain bone mass, and bone density tests can tell you if there's a problem before a broken bone occurs.

- **Arthritis.** Severe arthritis can make every move painful, and can seriously affect a person's quality of life. Two of the most common forms of arthritis are osteoarthritis and rheumatoid arthritis. In osteoarthritis, the cartilage in the joints becomes very thin and frayed, causing the joints to swell. The hands, feet, back, hips, and knees are commonly affected. Rheumatoid arthritis affects the whole body, not just certain joints, because the immune system turns on the joints and attacks them. Symptoms of this form of arthritis include soreness similar to that when you have the flu, stiffness, aching joints, and fatigue. Arthritis is extremely common in elderly people, but shouldn't be accepted as a fact of aging. Have your parent examined by a physician to determine the extent of the disease and what may be done to help.

- **Emphysema.** This is a nasty, chronic lung disease, which affects almost 2 million Americans. The major cause of emphysema is long-term smoking, although some people who never smoked also get the disease. It's more common in men than women, although it's on the increase in females. Another serious lung disease is chronic bronchitis, which also is thought to be caused primarily by smoking. Symptoms of both these lung diseases include breathlessness, frequent colds that last a long time, and deep, mucous-producing coughs. These are serious diseases that require the care of a physician, so if you suspect your parent may have a lung disease, make sure he gets medical treatment.

- **Dementia.** Dementia is a disorder of the brain that results in the progressive loss of memory and other intellectual functions. It's much more serious than the occasional forgetfulness that most people experience as they get older. The main cause of dementia is Alzheimer's disease, which causes the brain to degenerate. Dementia can begin at any age, but is most common after age 65. When it strikes before age 65 it's called presenile dementia, when it occurs after age 65 it's called senile dementia. People who appear to have senile dementia may actually have a condition such as a chest infection or depression, which can cause similar symptoms. A doctor will do a physical exam, test the memory, and test other mental functions to determine whether a person's condition is dementia or another, underlying disorder.

- **Chronic sleep disorders.** A sleep disorder may not sound too serious, but can be devastating to the person suffering from it, and to a spouse or other person who lives in the house. Sleep disorders affect nearly half of all elderly people, and can cause them to be groggy, irritable, and even disoriented during the day. A sleep disorder can become a vicious cycle. Dad has trouble sleeping at night, and, as a result, spends a good part of the day napping. The daytime napping makes it even harder for him to sleep at night, and on it goes. In severe cases, Dad becomes really agitated, is sure that he won't be able to sleep at night, and gets extremely irritable. Often, pills prescribed to help him to sleep have some pretty nasty side effects.

- **Depression and substance abuse.** Depression can be difficult to diagnose, but, once it's been identified, it's extremely treatable. Many older people suffer from undiagnosed depression, either because they don't recognize the warning signs, or because they're ashamed to admit they may be experiencing a mental problem. Mental illness has a long history of shame, largely because we've only recently addressed and begun to understand it. The U.S. Department of Health and Human Services lists 12 symptoms of clinical depression: persistent sadness, anxiety, or empty mood; loss of interest or pleasure in ordinary activities, family, or friends; decreased energy or listlessness; sleep problems; eating problems that result in weight loss or gain; difficulty concentrating, remembering or making decisions; feelings of hopelessness; feelings of guilt or worthlessness; thoughts of suicide or dying; irritability; excessive crying; recurring aches and pains that won't go away. If your parent has some of these symptoms, ask her about to see her doctor to talk about how she's feeling. Her doctor can make a diagnosis and refer her to a psychologist or counselor if necessary. A combination of therapy and medication has proven to be effective in treating depression. Substance abuse, mostly alcohol or prescription drugs with older people, can be a result, or a signal, of depression. Be alert to signs of substance abuse if you suspect depression.

- **Anxiety disorders.** About one in every 10 adults who are 55 years or older suffer from some form of anxiety disorder that's severe enough to require medical treatment. The symptoms of an anxiety disorder are feelings of nervous tension, increased fearfulness, and excessive worrying. If you suspect such a disorder in your parent, urge him to talk to his physician about it. Just be careful if anti-anxiety drugs are prescribed. Many of them can be habit forming and have some nasty side effects.

There are other diseases and disorders that affect elderly people, as well, but these are some of the major ones. Hopefully, you can keep an eye on Mom and Dad's medical conditions, and get them help when they need it.

Financial Health is Another Major Concern

It's a simple fact that life is more difficult for people who don't have enough money, and, elderly people, who are susceptible to a variety of diseases and illnesses may depend on several medications, are especially vulnerable to the effects of poverty. A survey conducted by the Nutrition Screening Initiative, a coalition of thirty national health, medical, and aging organizations, showed that one in every four elderly patients were malnourished, although reasons other than poverty also contribute to that rate.

Even elderly people who have enough money to live comfortably can suffer adverse effects from worrying about whether their money will run out, or if they'll be able to maintain their current lifestyles. A poll of 382 elderly people in Florida showed that 38 percent of them thought that having to pay higher premiums for Medicare would be a big problem. Another 34 percent feared not being able to pay their monthly bills. Hopefully, your parents have planned well for their financial futures, and have enough money to live comfortably throughout their old age, regardless of what it entails.

If they haven't planned financially, you can help them. You'll learn a lot more about how to do that in rest of this book. For now, however, keep in mind the link between physical and mental health and financial health, and understand how concerns about one area can be directly related to the other. Be sensitive to your parents' worries concerning these topics, and willing to sit down and discuss those worries when necessary.

Chapter Two

Financial Planning—Better Sooner than Later

If you're lucky, your parents will have planned carefully for their retirements and will have sufficient financial resources to allow them to live comfortably after they stop working.

Maybe they'll start going on some of those trips they've dreamed about for years. They'll finally be able to visit Mom's cousins in Ireland or take that cruise to the Bahamas they've been reading about. They've always wanted to see the Grand Canyon—perhaps now is the time. Maybe they'll buy a condo in Florida or Arizona where they can escape when the winter cold sets in; maybe Dad will finally get his fishing boat, and Mom can join the tennis club.

If major trips, second homes, and leisure-filled lifestyles aren't in the financial picture for your parents, then hopefully they at least have enough money to maintain their current lifestyle and have some options about what they're able to do. Nobody likes to think about their parents worrying constantly about whether or not they can afford to go out to dinner now and then, much less if they'll be able to pay the phone bill this month or replace the water heater if it should break down.

Unfortunately, many older people have not planned financially, and are suffering because of it. According to the Metropolitan Life Insurance Company, the average American spends 18 years in retirement, but fewer than half have put money aside specifically for those years. If your parents fall into that category, you may be facing some serious challenges.

A friend who lives in Texas tells of the nightmarish situation he's currently facing with his parents, who live in South Carolina. His father, who worked as a salesman in a clothing store for his whole working life and saved practically nothing, is very ill with a degenerative brain disease. His mother, Jake reports, is resentful and discontented that she's had to change her lifestyle. She continues to spend more money than they can afford. Nearly broke now, Jake's parents are looking to him for financial help, even though he has a son in his second year of college and a daughter who will start college in a year.

Jake, a banker, struggles constantly with guilt and anxiety concerning the situation. He would like to help his parents, but feels a great obligation to meet the financial needs of his own family. In addition, he and his wife, a teacher, save as much money as they possibly can for their own retirement, due largely to what Jake's seen happening to his parents. He resents his parents for putting him in an uncomfortable situation, then feels guilty about his resentment. It's an extremely difficult situation for everyone involved, especially with Jake's father being so sick. And, it's a situation that was caused by insufficient—or in this case—a complete lack of financial planning.

Most of us may never face the unfortunate situation that Jake does. But, many of us will have to address financial issues confronting our parents. They might need help figuring out how to pay for health care (more about that in Chapter Three), or deciding whether or not to buy long-term care insurance. Maybe they're looking for advice about selling their home, getting a reverse mortgage, tax issues, or rearranging some of their investments. They might need some help with estate planning. Having a good understanding of their financial situation makes it much easier to assist them with these types of issues when it becomes necessary.

Assessing Your Parents' Financial Situation

It's difficult to help someone with something that you don't understand. Remember the first time that your son or daughter came to you for help with that math problem that looked like it was written in Greek? You couldn't explain it, because you didn't get it. Or when you tried to assemble the new gas grill and hoped to grill some steaks that evening? It's not that you didn't want to help, you didn't have a clue where to begin.

Before you can help your parents with their financial issues, you need to make an assessment of their financial situation. This is the only way you can really know what they have, what they need, and what their options might be. You'll need to get a clear understanding of their assets and liabilities. You'll need to know what income they may have, what their expenses are, and what money they have available for various needs.

Remember that for many people—and especially older ones—money is very connected to feelings of independence, control and self worth. Those feelings, and other attitudes concerning money, can make discussing your parents' financial issues touchy. Be sensitive to their feelings and tread lightly whenever possible.

Is there enough money, for instance, if one of them should require home health care or have to go to a nursing home? Do they have the resources necessary to pay for their regular medications? If they pay rent or have a mortgage, how do those payments affect the balance of their available money? Will they have to sell their home in order to meet their expenses? You might be pleasantly surprised and find out that Mom and Dad have stashed away quite a bit over the years in various accounts and investments. Or, you might be dismayed to learn that they have very little, and the future is looking rather bleak. Either way, however, it's better to know than not to know.

Have They Planned Financially?

Ideally, financial planning for retirement should start the day a person lands his very first job. Realistically, it usually doesn't.

Retirement planning is a process that helps a person determine how much money he'll need to see him through the years after he stops working. It also lays out a plan for the best ways to save and accumulate money. Unfortunately, many people hardly think about funding their retirements until they're ready to retire, by which time it's too late to start saving adequate amounts.

We all know that hindsight is 20-20, and there are things in our lives we wish we'd done differently. Many people who have retired say one of their regrets is not having saved more money, and not having planned financially.

Studies show that most people need at least three-quarters as much money to maintain their standard of living during retirement as they required while working. This varies, of course, depending on factors such as health, location, and so forth. Social Security benefits for the average retiree are about 40 percent of their pre-retirement earnings. As you can see, there's a large gap between what Social Security provides and what it costs to live in retirement. If a retired person doesn't have enough money saved to make up the difference, there's a big problem.

Social Security is the primary source of income for about 66 percent of elderly Americans. And, experts say the rate of dependency is unlikely to drop in the future because of low savings rates.

It's easy to understand why retirement planning gets pushed to the back burner during the years in which a person is working. Paying the monthly bills, buying a house and a couple of cars, saving money to send kids to college, funding vacations, paying for orthodontists and sports camps, paying for weddings—immediate financial needs make it difficult to think about what will happen 20 or 30 years down the road. Only one-third of people who are working report that they've even tried to figure out how much money they'll need to have enough for a comfortable retirement.

Even among people who have planned financially for retirement, there are some common problems:

- Overestimating the rate at which savings will grow. Many people assume their savings will grow at a higher rate than at what really occurs, and are disappointed at retirement to learn their savings aren't worth as much as they'd anticipated.
- Underestimating life expectancy. People tend to believe they'll live about as long as their parents did. The life expectancy in this country, however, continues to increase, with many people living longer than they believed they would. The average life expectancy today gives a 65-year-old man an additional 15.6 years, and a 65-year-old woman an additional 19.2 years.
- Underestimating health care costs. Just because we're living longer doesn't mean we're necessarily living healthier. Many people don't count on the high costs of medications and services not covered by their insurance.

Financial planning is difficult, there's no question about it. Suppose your dad figured that he'd live an additional 15 years after retirement, but ends up living 25? Granted, it sounds like a good problem, but if he's saved only enough money to see him through 15 years, what will he live on for the other 10? Or, what if Mom is living very comfortably in a nice, affordable apartment, when she suffers a stroke and needs to move into an assisted living center? All of a sudden, her monthly living expenses increase dramatically, while her savings accounts do exactly the opposite.

If you spend any time with people who have been retired for a while, you'll probably notice a recurring theme. Many, many people who thought they had enough money saved for a comfortable retirement are sadly surprised to realize how quickly their savings are being used up, and terribly afraid of what will happen when those savings are gone.

Hopefully, we're all being smarter about our retirement planning—loading up our 401(k)s and individual retirement accounts to see us through our golden years. And, with luck, your parents also planned and saved for their retirement. To determine whether or not this has occurred, you'll need to do some investigating.

Knowing What They Have and What They Need

If you're going to be assisting your parents with their finances, it's important to know what they have, and what they need.

Estimate Mom and Dad's net worth by figuring out the total value of their assets, then subtracting the total value of their liabilities. A chart to help you keep track of these numbers is provided at the end of this chapter. Assets are wide ranging, including the following:

- Cash accounts
- Stocks and bonds
- Certificates of deposit
- Mutual funds
- Savings bonds
- Tax refunds
- Cash value life insurance
- Annuities
- IRAs
- Keogh accounts
- Businesses owned
- Cars
- Personal property/collectibles
- Mortgages owned
- Residence
- Income property
- Vacation home
- Potential inheritances

Liabilities include the following:
- Bank loans
- Car loans
- Credit card bills
- Home improvement loans
- Life insurance loans
- Mortgage
- Capital gains tax
- Income tax
- Property tax
- Alimony
- Personal loans

Once you've got an idea of their net worth, calculate their current monthly income, including pensions, Social Security payments, income from a property, and income from securities or retirement accounts.

Then, add up their current monthly expenses. These would include mortgage or rent, utilities, maintenance costs on the home, grocery bills, medical costs, entertainment, transportation, insurance premiums, clothing, travel, and so forth.

If you can see that your folks are spending more than they have coming in, you can calculate how much of their savings they're spending every month, and how long their savings will last. If their financial outlook is not rosy, you may need to help them figure out how they might trim their expenses or find some additional sources of income. You might even help them to set up a budget, so that they'll know exactly where their money is going, and how much they can afford to spend.

Your parents may be reasonable, thrifty, and frugal, and perfectly willing to cut back their spending in order to stretch their savings. If that's the case, count your blessings. If they're resistant to changing their lifestyle, even just a little bit in the interest of saving some money—your job will be more difficult.

Helping Your Parents Improve Their Financial Outlook

If you can see that your parent or parents are facing a difficult financial future, try to help them understand the situation. They might not realize how quickly their savings are being depleted, or the implications of running out of money.

If they're receptive to having you work with them to improve their financial position, there are several areas to explore.

Look first at where your parents' money is going. If there's credit card debt, find a way to pay it off as soon as possible, and encourage them to start buying on a cash-only basis. Check to see if the utility bills seem unusually high. If they are, look at the appliances they've been using. Old, non energy-efficient refrigerators, freezers, and other appliances can cause huge drains on electricity and increase utility bills substantially. If this is the case, consider exchanging the appliance for a different one, possibly a used one.

Older people tend not to be the main culprits when it comes to wracking up credit card debt, but with more than 60 million households in the United States carrying balances that average between $6,000 and $7,000, it probably wouldn't hurt to take a look at Mom's Visa bill.

If spending for medical costs seems out of balance, look at how much your parents are spending on medications. The cost of prescription drugs rose by 17.4 percent in 2000, totally out of whack with a less-than 2 percent inflation rate. If their drug bills are causing budget problems for your parents, explore the possibility of using generic drugs, or talk to their doctor about changing to a less expensive medication. Generic drugs can cost only half as much as brand names, and they must be approved by the Food and Drug Administration as being equivalent. You don't, of course, want to compromise Mom and Dad's health care, but doctors sometimes can find a drug with equal benefits for a much lower cost. Also, to minimize what can be expensive visits to the doctor's office, keep in mind that many churches, synagogues, senior centers, clinics, and even grocery stores offer flu shots at minimal cost. And, look for health fairs at local hospitals and schools that offer blood pressure checks, cholesterol screenings, and so forth. If either parent is a veteran, be sure to look into veteran's benefits (more about that in Chapter Three).

Don't overlook obvious areas of possible overspending, such as clothing, frequent dinners at expensive restaurants, or other entertainment costs. These are easy areas in which to reduce spending. Another possibility is that Mom and Dad are giving money to a child or grandchild, either out of simple generosity, or because they feel the child or grandchild needs some help.

Another place to look for reducing expenses is your parents' insurance policies. It's not unheard of for someone to keep paying on a policy that is no longer necessary. Check for old policies or redundant coverage that might be driving up insurance costs. If Dad still has a term life insurance policy, he's probably paying pretty outrageous premiums, and should look into changing to a cash value plan. You'll read more about different types of insurance in Chapter Three.

If your folks are controlling expenses, but still find themselves digging heavily into their savings accounts each month to pay their bills, you may be able to discover some additional means of income for them.

If they're still living in the home in which they raised their children, or another home that has more space than they really need, it's possible that the value of the home has increased dramatically and they could make a significant profit by selling it. Remember that since 1997, the capital gains exclusion on the sale of a home is $500,000 for a couple and $250,000 for a single person. If they don't want to give up their home, they might consider renting a room or apartment for the additional income.

Mom and Dad also may be able to use a home equity conversion (HEC) plan to get a lump sum or a regular flow of cash. HEC loans usually do not have to be repaid until the home is sold or your parents move or die. There are eligibility requirements for this type of loans. The requirements are based on age, income, assets, need, value of the home, and any outstanding debts or mortgages.

The most common type of HEC loan is known as a reverse mortgage. A reverse mortgage, simply put, is when a lender pays the homeowner a monthly payment, with the idea that the lender will be repaid after the property is sold. It's the opposite of a traditional mortgage, in which the person living in the home pays a monthly rate with the goal of eventually owning the property. A reverse mortgage, which are available in most states through a bank or agency, may be an option if your parents own their home outright, or have only a small balance on their current mortgage.

There are several types of reverse mortgages, including those that are federally insured, those that are uninsured, and one called a reverse annuity mortgage. Each type includes advantages and disadvantages. Other home-related avenues to explore are home repair loans, which provide a one-time, no or low-interest loan for home repairs or approved improvements; sale-leaseback plans, which allows a person to sell a home but remain living there as a tenant; and property-tax deferral loans, which allows an elderly person to defer paying property tax. The tax, plus interest, however, must be paid when the house is sold, or when the elderly person moves or dies.

Reverse mortgages are available through the Department of Housing and Urban Development (HUD); the American Association of Retired Persons (AARP) offers a pamphlet and video about reverse mortgages. You can call HUD at 1-888-466-3487, and contact AARP at 800-424-3410. AARP can be found online at www.aarp.org.

Borrowing money under any circumstances is not something that should be done without careful consideration. It's probably best to consult a lawyer to make sure that any borrowing arrangement is safe, especially when it involves your parent's home, which may be his or her only source of equity.

If you happen to have enough money, and your parents are willing to accept your help, it's perfectly fine for you to help them out financially. Most financial advisors, however, do not recommend giving Mom and Dad money at the expense of your own family or your retirement accounts. The idea of not helping your parents when you know you have money with which you could do so may be very unpleasant and difficult to accept. Remember, however, that by jeopardizing your own finances, you'll run the risk of being in the exact spot your parents are in now when you retire. If that happens, your children will be in the exact spot that you are now.

Talking Things Through

The best way for you to learn about your parents' financial situation is to sit down with them and talk about it. Ideally, they'll be willing to share information concerning their financial situation, and you'll be able to discuss their circumstances and get a clear picture of what's going on. Remember, however, that you're talking about matters that directly affect their lives and the lifestyles they know. Finances, especially when they're linked to a home or other important asset, can be an emotional topic.

When you sit down with your parent or parents to discuss financial matters, it's important to remain calm and matter-of-fact. Money is a sensitive subject with many people—and can be an especially tense topic for older men and women who are concerned about their financial futures. Your parents may realize that they need some financial guidance, but be reluctant for you to know the details of their financial situation. Remember that attitudes about money have changed greatly in the past 20 or 30 years. Talking about money used to be practically taboo, unless you were speaking with a banker, insurance agent, or car salesman. Money was a private matter, and not discussed in general conversation.

Your parents probably didn't include you in any financial discussions or decisions as you were growing up, and it may be difficult for them to do so now. Revealing the details of their finances to you may signify to them a beginning of a loss of independence, making them resistant to sharing financial information. You'll need to be sensitive to these, and any other feelings and attitudes that your parents might have that are associated with money.

If they are willing to discuss money matters, be careful not to appear to be judgmental or critical. You might explain basic financial tools and options, and then discuss with them what you think would be in their best interests. Don't, however, be overly critical of how they've handled their finances in the past. If your mother has every cent she owns in a savings account that's earning two and a half percent interest, for instance, you certainly want to tell her about some better options for her money. You don't, however, need to make her feel awful about what she's done up to this point. She may be distrustful of any other type of investment, or embarrassed because she never understood the concept of stocks and bonds.

If your parents refuse to let you in on their finances, try to be understanding. It may simply be too traumatic or difficult for them to discuss their personal money matter with their child. If they flatly refuse to discuss anything remotely related to finances, you could suggest that they see a financial planner or lawyer. You'll learn more about this later in this chapter.

Sometimes, an older parent may be so reluctant to discuss financial matters or problems that he'll get into serious money trouble while trying to handle a situation that is too complex or difficult. There have been many cases in which grown children have no idea that a parent can no longer afford to pay rent or medical expenses, simply because the parent refuses to talk about it. If that should happen, point out very clearly what will happen if Mom doesn't pay her rent that month, and offer to help her figure out a solution to the problem. It may be that she doesn't fully realize the seriousness of the situation, and will be glad for your help once she does.

Taking Charge of Your Parents' Finances

If your parent or parents is getting to the point where they can no longer handle their finances, you may have to address the issue of taking charge. You should know right up front that doing so will not be an easy or pleasant task. People who have taken control of their parents' finances usually report that it is an emotional struggle. But, sometimes, it's necessary.

Maybe you've noticed that Mom routinely forgets to record checks she's written, and her account is frequently overdrawn. Or that Dad can't seem to grasp his health insurance statements the way he used to. Perhaps a utility has been cut off because Dad forgot to pay the bill. Maybe you're upset that your parents ended up buying an expensive home security system after a salesperson called and warned them about the dangers of living unprotected in today's society. You worry about who will call next and what he'll be selling. All of these certainly are reasons to be concerned.

Knowing When It's Necessary

You might become aware that it's necessary for you, or someone else, to take over Dad's finances because he tells you that he can no longer do it. If that's the case, consider yourself lucky in some regards.

Having Dad admit that he can't handle the financial chores any more makes it easy for you to offer your help. Sometimes, though, Dad will insist he's capable of handling his own financial affairs, and you know that he's not.

If any of the scenarios mentioned in the previous section—unrecorded checks, account overdraws, trouble figuring out bills or statements, missed bill payments, trouble with telemarketers—have occurred with your parents, you probably can assume they need help handling their finances. If any of the scenarios occur regularly, you probably can assume that it's time for somebody to step in and take over, or, at the very least, provide assistance with their finances.

Avoiding Unnecessary Conflicts

If you're worried about Dad's capability to handle his financial affairs, sit down with him and suggest the he consider appointing an agent in a durable power of attorney. Explain to him that signing a power of attorney doesn't mean that he relinquishes all control of his finances. He's still in charge, but the person he appoints as his agent will help him and take care of the day-to-day chores such as paying the bills, sorting out the insurance statements, and making bank deposits. The topic of power of attorney will be covered in Chapter Three.

Losing control of his finances is likely to be a frightening thought for Dad, and you need to reassure him that you're not out to take his money, or remove his authority. Naming you as the agent in a durable power of attorney simply means that you'll help him, and that you'll act in his best interests if he's no longer to do so himself.

Be respectful of his feelings, and assure him that you will always follow his instructions concerning his finances and will work to benefit him. Try to get an idea of his financial goals and priorities, so you can anticipate what he'll want you to do with his money. Is he committed to saving as much as he can to pass along as inheritance to his children? Or does he want to spend the money he has in order to make his life comfortable and take some of the burden of care off his family? If money is tight, is he willing to consider some sort of public assistance? Remember that many older people are fiercely proud, and extremely resistant to the idea of any sort of "handout." Would he be interested in looking into getting a loan? What does he most need his money for? Having a clear understanding of these kinds of issues can make it easier down the road for you and your parent.

If your parent for any reason does not want to give power of attorney to a child or other family member, he can appoint a trusted lawyer or banker as his agent.

Involving Other Family Members

If you have brothers or sisters, be sure that you include them in any decisions you make concerning Mom's and Dad's finances. Nothing is likely to breed resentment as quickly as the notion that you're meddling in your parents' financial matters and keeping it a secret from your siblings.

Every family has its own relationships and dynamics. Be aware, however, that even the best relationships can become frayed in time of stress, and that caring for elderly parents can be a very stressful job. Mom and Dad can sometimes unwittingly contribute to strained sibling relationships by confiding in one child and excluding the others. If you happen to, for whatever reason, become their confidant, it's a good idea to share the contents with your siblings, unless your parents specifically ask you not to.

Although it often seems that one or two children end up doing the bulk of work in caring for elderly parents, it's important that all brothers and sisters are involved and informed about what's happening—financially and otherwise. Ideally, your brothers and sisters will be grateful that you're helping Mom and Dad handle what can sometimes be complicated issues. Just be sure to keep everyone in the loop regarding family financial issues.

Managing Financial Matters Online

If you do take over management of your parents' finances, it will entail a portion of your time and energy. If you're like most people, you're probably already busier than you'd care to be. It's a common lament that there aren't enough hours in a day or days in a week to accomplish all that needs to be done.

You might streamline the chores associated with managing your parents' finances by going online. Online banking, also known as electronic banking, home banking, Internet banking, or PC banking, allows you complete regular tasks from home, saving you from making trips to the bank, writing checks to pay bills, calling the bank to check an account balance, and so forth. It's particularly useful when you live in one city or town and your parent or parents in another. Online banking, with you having access to your parents' accounts, allows you to handle financial matters anytime—from any place. Some of the services offered online include:

- Check account balances
- Transfer funds from one account to another
- Pay monthly bills
- Apply for loans
- Download information about accounts
- Trade stocks or mutual funds
- Order and reorder checks
- View images of checks and deposits

Not all banks offer all these online services, but options for consumers are increasing as more and more people log on to Internet banking. Electronic banking is an option, even if you don't have Internet access. Some banks are set up for customers to use money management software and their own computers to access their accounts using a modem and phone line. Other institutions, such as Telebank and Net.B@nk, are completely contained on the Internet, and are frequently referred to as Internet-only banks. No special software is required for Internet-only banks, and, because they're less expensive to operate than traditional banks, they're often able to pass along savings to customers in terms of fees and other costs. Traditional banks that offer an online banking option may require special software for customers to be able to bank electronically.

Many people are hesitant about Internet banking because of security concerns, or fear that it will be too complicated or confusing. Online banking still is fairly new, but increasing numbers of people are using it, most of them without any problems. Many people who use online banking—either to manage their own accounts or those of their parents—say they don't know how they'd manage without it. Banks that offer online banking normally have websites that are explicit about the services offered, how to sign on for online banking, and so forth. And, you can always call the bank and talk to a customer service representative if you have problems.

Signing on for online banking with a traditional bank normally is pretty straightforward. You'll need to provide some information to verify that you are, indeed, an account holder. And, you may need to choose a software program such as Quicken that will give you access to your bank's online services. If you go with an Internet-only bank, you'll most likely be asked to print out a registration form you'll find on the bank's web site, fill it out, sign it, and mail it to the bank.

Be sure to spend some time at an Internet-only bank's web site before signing on with it. Does it seem like it will be easy to work with? Does the site contain instructions that are clearly defined and understandable? Check out the contact information and make sure you'll be able to get customer help if you need it. If there's a phone number listed, call and see how long it takes you to get through to someone.

Banks that offer online services employ tight security measures to protect their customers' information and accounts. Some of those measures include displaying only a portion of a customer's account number on the screen, and automatic logoff if no action is taken within an account for a specified period of time (usually 10 or 15 minutes) during which the account is in use. Customers are required to use an I.D. and password for access to their accounts, and banks monitor their systems to prevent problems that could interfere with security.

To learn more about online banking, you can contact someone at your bank, or check out some websites that will get you acquainted with this new way of conducting bank business. Some websites that can get you started are listed below:

- Bank of America at www.bankofamerica.com/onlinebanking
- Chase Manhattan Bank at www.chase.com
- Fleet Bank at www.fleet.com
- Citibank at www.citibank.com
- Sovereign Bank at www.sovereignbank.com

Or check out the Bank Web, which is a listing of hundreds of banks offering online services. Banks are listed by state, and you can connect with any of them from this site. Bank Web is located at www.bankweb.com.

There's another, fairly new service that might be helpful if you're taking care of bill paying for your folks. Independent bill paying services allow you to receive and pay your bills online. That means that, once arrangements have been made, you could receive and review their bills on line, select a payment date, and authorize the payment of the amount due. There's a fee for this service, of course—usually somewhere between $8 and $10 a month. Still, you may decide the cost is well worthwhile.

A couple of these services are Paytrust and PayMyBills. You can learn more about them from their web sites at www.paytrust.com and www.paymy-bills.com.

Gathering and Organizing Legal and Financial Information

Our lives sometimes seem to be overrun by paperwork. Papers accumulate in every room of the house—sign-up sheets for the kids' sports programs and other activities, school papers, bills that need to be paid, bank account and other account statements—you get the picture. While many of these papers are more clutter than content, some papers are extremely important.

Whether you're already a caregiver for your aging parents, or just thinking about the possibility of caring for them some day, it's extremely important that you have some important legal and financial information available. Having certain financial records and other information such as insurance policies, the names of their doctors and lawyers, copies of their wills, and identification numbers for their Social Security and Medicare policies can save a lot of trouble and anxiety down the road.

Doing It Now to Avoid a Future Crisis

Nobody likes to think about a parent getting sick or becoming disabled. When our parents are well, we tend to assume that they'll stay that way forever. It's easier, and a lot more pleasant, to cross our fingers and wish for continued good fortune than to take a hard, realistic look at some rather grim possibilities for the future.

Nobody benefits, though, if you bury your head in the sand and refuse to consider what may lie ahead as far as your parents are concerned. Doing so leaves you woefully unprepared to deal with caring for your parents, and it denies them the opportunity to tell you what they expect and desire for the future.

If your parents are very elderly, or your dad's just been diagnosed with cancer or your mom's had a heart attack, the urgency to organize and plan can increase tremendously. When everything's going along smoothly, however, we tend to put off talking about difficult subjects or dealing with what seem like unpleasant tasks.

A recent study by the Kaiser Family Foundation showed that forty-five percent of adults who say their elderly parent has a regular physician don't know the doctor's name. Forty-three percent know little or nothing about their parents' health insurance.

It's far easier to deal with topics such as writing a will, dwindling bank accounts, or considering buying long-term insurance when a parent or parents are reasonably well and healthy. Most people find it's much more difficult to broach the subject of a will with someone who's just been diagnosed with a terminal illness than with someone who's healthy. It's much less emotional and less upsetting to talk about such topics before it becomes absolutely necessary. A woman confided after her husband died that she never knew what kind of funeral he wanted because they never talked about such matters. It simply never seemed like an issue until he became very ill, and after that she didn't feel she could talk to him about it because it was too painful and difficult to broach.

Putting off the task of gathering legal and financial information that pertains to your parents puts you at risk for a crisis in the event that one or both of them becomes ill or incapacitated.

Consider the possibility that both your parents could be severely injured in a car accident. No, it's not pleasant to think about, but accidents happen every day, and many of them involve older drivers. Should such a thing occur, you could have both parents in a hospital—Mom with major, but non-critical injuries, and Dad on life support. Imagine the helplessness of not knowing if Dad has a living will or durable power of attorney for health care, or what Mom's health insurance might or might not cover.

A couple, both in their late 70s, was vacationing in New England when the woman had a stroke. She was admitted to a hospital there and appeared to be recovering, when she took a serious downturn and was transported by helicopter to a larger, city hospital. Her daughters arrived shortly before she fell into a coma and all her major organs began shutting down. It was a great comfort for her husband and daughters to be able to contact the woman's lawyer and have a copy of her living will faxed to the hospital. Knowing from the living will that their wife and mother wanted no extraordinary measures taken to keep her alive made it much easier for them to make the hard decisions they had to make during the last hours of her life.

If you haven't already obtained and organized the important information and papers pertaining to your parents' legal and financial matters, it's time to get busy. You need to get this material organized and in a place where you can access it easily when it becomes necessary.

Assuring That You Have the Information You Need

If you're lucky, your parents will have thought about the possibility of one of them becoming ill or impaired, and will already have organized their financial and legal information. But, you shouldn't assume that they've done so. About 70 percent of people in the United States do not have even a basic will, and even fewer have documents such as living wills.

If they're both alive, approach the subject with your parents and remind them that it's very important that everything is organized and accessible to the other one. That way, if Mom suddenly becomes very sick, Dad doesn't have to make a difficult situation even more difficult by having to search around for documents and information.

If one parent has already died, you could offer to help the other round up all the necessary documents. If Dad says he doesn't need your help, write down what information you need, and tell him he'd be doing you a big favor by getting it all together and in a place where you could get your hands on it if you should you need it. Be sure to follow up in a few weeks to see if he's taken any action.

If one parent has already died and the other is ill or incapacitated, you might have to gather the information by yourself. This is the least desirable alternative, because it means you're going to have to dig through Dad's personal papers to find what you need. This might be a time to call a brother, sister, or close friend to come in and give you a hand. Not only would it be good moral support to have some company while performing a difficult task, it would give you some backup in the possible event that a family member would later come back and accuse you or snooping or meddling in Dad's personal affairs.

If you're trying to find information on your own, you might try calling the agencies and companies with which your parents have dealt. Some are willing to share information concerning a client's account or policy with family members, while others are not. The only thing you can do is to explain why you need the information and hope for the best.

If you find that you need to organize financial and legal information without your parents' help, start by looking at a copy of their most recent federal income tax return. Be sure to call their lawyer, accountant, financial advisor, and anyone else who may have knowledge about necessary documents or information. If you know where they keep information pertaining to their finances and legal matters, you'll need to look through files to find what you need. Don't forget that there may be information stored in a safe deposit box or lock box.

Ideally, you won't find it too difficult to pull together the legal and financial information that you need. Once you have it, make sure you put it in a safe, accessible place, and tell your siblings where it is.

Information You Need to Have

Having stated the importance of gathering pertinent financial and legal information, it's time to take a look at what that packet of information should include. Some of the items listed may not apply to your parents, depending on their circumstances. All of these topics will be discussed in more detail in later chapters.

- Your parent or parents' will. Make sure you also have any codicils that may have been added. Codicils are changes or additions made to the original will.
- Living will. A living will is a legal document that states your parents' wishes about their medical care in the event that they are terminally ill or injured, or are permanently unconscious. A living will focuses primarily on end-of-life issues.
- Medical power of attorney. A medical power of attorney also is a legal document concerning medical care, but does not focus primarily on end-of-life issues. It appoints an agent who is authorized to make decisions in the event that your parent is incapacitated can not make decisions for himself concerning issues such as medical records, hospital admissions, and transfers from one facility to another.

- General power of attorney. If your parent has appointed a power of attorney, there will be a legal document to that effect.
- Numbers and identification cards for Social Security, Medicare, and Medicaid.
- All information regarding various insurance policies your parents may have. This includes their health insurance, disability, homeowner's, auto, personal property, credit card, and so forth. Find out who is the agent for each policy.
- The locations and account numbers for all savings, checking, and money market accounts.
- A list of all stocks, bonds, and other securities that your parent or parents owns.
- Retirement account information, including 401(k)s, IRAs, Roth IRAs, Keoghs, SEP IRAs, and so forth.
- Pension plan identification and information.
- Deeds to all real estate.
- Other information concerning real estate, such as rental agreements, maintenance agreements on vacation homes, and so forth.
- Titles to all vehicles, including trailers, boats, and so forth.
- Information regarding any business ventures in which a parent may be involved. Perhaps your dad still owns part of the business he used to run, or Mom had started a part-time pet-care service.
- Debts. Including those on credit cards, unpaid bills, mortgages, home improvement loans, and auto loans.
- A list of routine monthly or quarterly bills, such as for electricity, heating, telephone, water, trash, cable television, and insurance premiums. You'll need this in the event that you take over bill paying.
- Copies of all tax returns—federal, state and local—for at least the past three years.
- Receipts for large, recent expenditures, such as property taxes or insurance premiums.
- The locations of valuable items. Many people hide valuables to protect them, sometimes forgetting where they placed them. If your parent is unable to tell you if anything is hidden, it might be worth a search. Many a $100 bill has been found in between the pages of a book. Try to identify valuable items that your parent owns, such as a set of sterling silver or jewelry, and think about where she might have stashed it.

- Keys. Including house keys, car keys, and those to safe deposit boxes, post office boxes, rental properties, vacation homes, garages, and so forth.
- Names, locations, and phone numbers. It may be important to be able to get in touch with certain people quickly. Have this information available for your parent's doctors, lawyer, financial advisor, accountant, insurance agent, and bank. You also could include other health-care providers such as the dentist and eye doctor, home health-care workers, physical therapists, and the pharmacy where Mom buys her medications.

You may think of other information you want to include. Every person's list will be different, but the items listed above can serve as a starting point. Once you've assembled all the necessary information regarding financial and legal matters, you might want to organize a little further.

If you're already caring for an ill parent in her home, or have a parent in the hospital, or are helping a parent who can no longer keep up the demands of keeping a house, it's a good idea to make a list that includes things such as what day the trash gets picked up, the recycling schedule, regularly scheduled service visits such as lawn care, and your mom's regular doctor appointments. Care giving is hard work, and anything you can do to keep yourself organized will be beneficial.

Caring for a parent or parents, and maybe their home, while trying to manage your own life, job, and home is an extremely difficult chore. Don't be surprised, or critical of yourself if you feel overwhelmed. And, don't hesitate to ask a sibling or friend for help when you need it. Having legal, financial, medical and practical information available and easily accessible should be a comfort to everyone, and can go a long way in making a tough situation more manageable.

Getting Help When You Need It

If you're caring for an elderly parent, there will be times when you need some help. It might be only that you need somebody to come and sit with you for moral support, or you might need expert legal or financial advice.

Fortunately, there is help available in nearly all areas of care giving. There's a lot more information about support groups and other resources in Chapter Five, so for now we'll focus on finding help with financial and legal issues. Some circumstances that might prompt you to seek advice from a professional include those listed below.

- Your parents have significant assets. In 2001, any assets over $1 million were subject to state and federal "death" taxes. The figure will increase to $2 million, and other changes are pending due to the recent tax package. Regulations concerning death taxes are changing, and it's important that you find someone dependable who can help you reduce the impact they'll have on you and your family.
- Your mother is just about at the point where she'll be eligible for Medicaid, and you want to see about the possibility of protecting some of her assets and advancing her eligibility for benefits.
- Mom and Dad's finances are in pretty much of a mess. You've suggested that they sit down with someone and try to figure out how to maximize their assets while better controlling their spending.
- Your dad died six months ago, and Mom hasn't taken any steps toward updating her will.
- Your dad has documentation concerning his pension plan that states he should be getting $145 a month more than he is. Representatives of his former company refuse to talk with him about it.
- Dad has his hand in two or three different businesses, and doesn't seem quite sure what his share is. He also owns some real estate associated with the businesses.

The obvious place to start if you think you need some help is with your parents' own lawyers and financial advisors. They may have had the same lawyer for years and years, and he knows them quite well. If they've worked closely with a financial advisor or accountant, that person will have access to their finances and can be a great help when you're trying to gather and organize information.

If your parents don't have their own lawyer or financial advisor, and for one reason or another many people do not, you might need to find someone to assist. You could go to your lawyer or financial advisor, or you could try another avenue.

The aging population is growing quickly, and new services have become available to meet its needs. Some of those services include advocacy for elderly people, financial firms that specialize in retirement planning and other financial issues affecting older people, and elder law attorneys.

Advocacy Services

Taking care of an elderly parent can be extremely demanding, time consuming, and emotionally draining. It also can entail a great deal of filling out forms; trying to figure out medical reports, insurance bills and statements; and working to get all the benefits and help to which your parent is entitled.

Advocacy services for the elderly can help with chores such as completing forms and contacting insurance companies with questions about coverage—or lack of coverage. They also can locate the best nursing homes in a particular area, arrange for home health care or therapy, and make sure an elderly person has a suitable place to live. Such service agencies are extremely popular in areas with large concentrations of elderly people who live away from their families, such as in Florida, where many elderly people move when they retire.

Marge Gibbons is a geriatric care manager who owns and operates Assist America, Inc., an advocacy agency in Largo, Florida. She says one of the primary advantages to hiring an advocacy service to help with issues involving aging parents is that parents tend to be more receptive to suggestions from professionals than to advice from their own children.

Gibbons, whose agency is approved by the National Association of Professional Geriatric Care Managers, arranges for any type of service necessary to resolve a problem situation. It's usually a family member, not the elderly person himself, who contacts her for help.

"When someone contacts me, it's almost always due to a problem situation," Gibbons says. "I'll go and assess the situation, and then determine the needs and the wishes of both the client (the elderly person) and the sponsor (the family member)."

Because she knows what services are available and where to find them, Gibbons, who says families can expect to pay between $50 and $125 an hour for the services of a geriatric care manager, can arrange for the necessary care much faster and more easily than a family member could.

"I know the resources, and I shop the resources that they need and can afford," Gibbons says. "I can do in three phone calls what it may take someone else three days to accomplish."

Senior-Specialized Financial Services and Elder Law Attorneys

There also are a growing number of financial firms and lawyers that specialize in issues that are pertinent to elderly people.

These financial advisors' expertise is in areas such as making the most of money saved for retirement, tax advantages for older people, estate planning, and other matters that relate directly to seniors. To find one of these firms, check your local phone book, or call a senior center or area office for the aging.

Relatively new to the legal profession (within the past 10 years or so) are elder law attorneys. Elder law attorneys specialize in matters such as estate planning, probate, and the administration and management of trusts. They appeal denials of Social Security, Medicare and Medicaid benefits, or work on the client's behalf to settle insurance claims.

Some of the services offered by elderly advocacy firms, senior-specialized financial service firms and elder law attorneys are likely to overlap. Be sure that you don't end up hiring a lawyer to solve a social service or health care problem. Check out the various types of agencies and the services they offer before hiring one.

Elder law attorneys handle matters concerning retirement and pension benefits, survivor benefits, living wills, durable power of attorney, and guardianships. If you suspect that your parent has been the victim of fraud or some kind of scam, or may have been abused, an elder law attorney probably can help.

As important as their knowledge of the legal matters that affect the elderly is, elder law attorneys also are known to be understanding and compassionate when working with older people. They are trained to work with the elderly, and have a good grasp of problems that particularly affect that age group. Elder care attorneys will treat your parent with respect and consideration while helping them solve any legal problems they may have encountered.

Elder care attorneys may be new to your area and relatively unknown. To find one, try calling a local association such as your area office for the aging, the Alzheimer's Association, AARP chapter, or the local senior center. Or, call the bar association in your area and ask for a listing of lawyers and their areas of specialty. There also is a National Association of Elder Law Attorneys, which provides of list of all the elder law attorneys in the country. You can access it on the Internet at www.naela.com, or by mail at 1604 North Country Club Road, Tucson, AZ 85716. The phone number for the association is 520-325-7925.

If you're going to pay an advocate, financial advisor, or lawyer, you want to find the best one you possibly can. There are many, many financial advisors and lawyers in this country—most of them very good at what they do, and some not so good. When contacting one of these specialists about a particular problem, you should briefly describe the situation about which you're calling. The advocate, advisor, or lawyer will ask you some questions about your parent and his circumstances. When she's finished with her questions, it's time for you to ask some of your own. Questions to consider asking include the following.

- How have you prepared for this job? This is an especially important question for advocates for the elderly. Many advocates have education and training that specifically relates to caring for older people and the issues that many of them face, but some may have no specific training at all. It's also a good question to ask a financial advisor. There are various categories of financial advisors, ranging from uncertified financial planners to highly trained and certified money managers.
- How long have you been in this business? Although some of the best and brightest lawyers, financial advisors, and advocates probably are just starting out, there's something to be said for experience when it comes to dealing with your parents and the problems that pertain specifically to older people.
- Did you have another career before becoming an advocate/financial advisor/lawyer? Look for a logical progression if the person has changed careers. A home health care provider becoming an advocate for elderly people is a natural move, spurred by experience from the previous job and probably a good dose of compassion. Same for a trust officer in a bank becoming a financial advisor. But you'd have to wonder about the progression if the advocate you're thinking about hiring turned out to have been a nail stylist or vacuum cleaner salesman before taking up the cause of the elderly.
- How long have you specialized in issues pertaining to older people? A lawyer may tell you she's been practicing for 15 years, but it could be that she's only specialized in elder law for the past three months. If you don't ask, you won't know.
- What percentage of your practice is dedicated to working with older people? A financial advisor might specialize in working with elderly people, but have most of his business with people in their 40s. Same for an elder law attorney.
- After you've described the problem or issue that your parent is facing, you should ask some specific questions pertaining to how the person you hire will address and handle the issue facing you and your parent. Those questions would include the following.

- What ideas do you have for solving my parent's problem? It's okay if your prospective employee says he'll want to further research the issue before telling you exactly how he'll handle it, but he should at least know with whom he'll be dealing and have a general plan on how to handle the problem.
- How much time do you expect it will take to handle this matter? You probably won't get an exact figure, but you'll at least have an idea if resolving the matter will take a couple of hours, a few days, or several weeks.
- Can you give me an estimate of what it will cost for you to handle this matter? Again, you won't get an exact amount, but the lawyer/financial advisor/advocate should be able to give you a ballpark figure. Also find out if an advance payment is required, and how often the professional sends out bills. Does he charge for time spent with you on the telephone? Does he have an hourly rate, or work on commission or charge a flat fee?
- Will you handle this case yourself, or will you have other people helping you? If there will be other people involved, ask about their training, experience, and areas of expertise. If she plans to use assistants on your case, their fee should be lower than that of the primary person.
- Can you predict whether or not you'll be successful in resolving this problem? If you're facing an unusually tough situation, don't automatically discount someone who tells you that she can't guarantee success. It's better that she's honest with you than just telling you what you want to hear, and, just because she can't guarantee success doesn't mean she necessarily will fail.

Once you've asked and received satisfactory answers to your questions, take a little time to think about what you've heard, and to compare the answers with those of other professionals with whom you've spoken. You don't need to tell someone immediately that you plan to hire him. It's also within your right to ask for the names of some other clients, preferable those with circumstances that are similar to your own, so you can call them and get their opinion of the person you're thinking about hiring.

Legal and financial problems are extremely important to your parent, and you want to be sure that you find someone with whom he can work effectively and comfortably. Keep Dad informed while you search for someone to represent him. Share the information you've obtained, and ask for his input, if he's able to give it. Once you've done your homework and obtained as much information as possible about the professional you're considering hiring, trust your instincts. Experience and reputation are important, but it's also important that you feel comfortable with the person you plan to hire. You should feel that the person is caring and honest, and will do her very best to help you and your parent.

Checklist of Assets and Liabilities

List your parents' assets and liabilities in the spaces below, as accurately as possible. Then subtract the total of the liabilities from the total of the assets to determine net worth.

Assets:

Cash accounts (savings and checking) $ _____

Stocks and bonds (total value) $ _____

Certificates of deposit $ _____

Mutual funds $ _____

Savings bonds $ _____

Tax refunds $ _____

Cash value life insurance $ _____

Annuities $ _____

IRAs $ _____

Keogh accounts $ _____

Personal Property

Businesses owned $ _____

Cars $ _____

Personal property/collectibles $ _____

Real Estate

Mortgages owned $ _____

Residence $ _____

Income property $ _____

Vacation home $ _____

TOTAL $ _____

Liabilities:

Bank loans $ _____

Car loans $ _____

Credit card bills $ _____

Home improvement loans $ _____

Life insurance loans $ _____

Mortgage $ _____

Alimony $ _____
Personal loans $ _____
Miscellaneous liabilities $ _____
Tax Liabilities
Capital gains tax $ _____
Income tax $ _____
Property tax $ _____

TOTAL $ _____

TOTAL ASSETS $ _____
LESS TOTAL LIABILITIES $ _____
EQUALS TOTAL NET WORTH $ _____

Checklist of Monthly Income and Expenses

List your parents' monthly income and expenses in the spaces below, as accurately as possible. Then, subtract the total of the expenses from the total of the income to determine their financial situation.

Income:

Pensions	$ _____
Social Security payments	$ _____
Real Estate Income	$ _____
Securities	
Retirement Accounts	$ _____
Alimony	$ _____
Personal income	$ _____
TOTAL	$ _____

Expenses:

Mortgage or Rent	$ _____
Utilities	$ _____
Home Maintenance	$ _____
Groceries	$ _____
Insurance Premiums	$ _____
Medical Costs	$ _____
Entertainment	$ _____
Transportation	$ _____
Travel	$ _____
Clothing	$ _____
Miscellaneous	$ _____
TOTAL	$ _____
TOTAL INCOME	$ _____
TOTAL EXPENSES	$ _____

Checklist of Important Items and Documents

Below is a checklist of items and documents to which you should have access if it would be necessary. Be sure you know where each of these items is located and how to get it when needed.

Your parent or parents' will and any codicils (changes or additions) _____

Living will or wills _____

Medical power of attorney _____

General power of attorney _____

Numbers and identification cards for Social Security, Medicare, and Medicaid

_____

Information (including agent) on all insurance policies (health, auto, home, etc.) _____

Locations and numbers for all bank accounts (savings, checking, money market) _____

List of all stocks, bonds, and other securities owned by your parents _____

Retirement account information _____

Pension plan identification and information _____

Deeds to all real estate _____

Other information pertaining to real estate, such as rental agreements _____

Titles to all vehicles _____

Information about any business venture in which your parent is involved

_____

A record of debt (such as credit card, mortgage, auto loans, etc.) _____

List of routine monthly or quarterly bills _____

Copies of all federal, state, and local tax returns _____

Receipts for large, recent expenses such as property taxes or insurance premiums _____

Locations of all valuable items _____

Keys (house, car, safe deposit box, post office box, rental properties, etc.

_____

Names and phone numbers of all lawyers, doctors, neighbors, pharmacies, etc.

_____

Financial Record-Keeping

BANK ACCOUNTS:

Savings Accounts:

Bank Name: _____ Account Number: _____

Bank Name: _____ Account Number: _____

Checking Accounts:

Bank Name: _____ Account Number: _____

Bank Name: _____ Account Number: _____

Certificates of Deposit:

Bank Name: _____ Account Number: _____

Bank Name: _____ Account Number: _____

Money Market Accounts:

Bank Name: _____ Account Number: _____

Bank Name: _____ Account Number: _____

Safe Deposit Box:

Bank Name: _____ Box/Key Number: _____

STOCKS, BONDS, AND MUTUAL FUNDS:

Broker: _____ Account Number: _____

Investments: _____

_____

Broker: _____ Account Number: _____

Investments: _____

_____

Broker: _____ Account Number: _____

Investments: _____

_____

RETIREMENT PLANS:

Pension Account Number: _____

IRA Accounts: _____

Bank Name: _____ Account Number: _____

Bank Name: _____ Account Number: _____

Keogh Plans: _____

Bank/Co. Name: _____ Account Number: _____

Bank/Co. Name: _____ Account Number: _____

Annuities:

Bank/Co. Name: _____ Account Number: _____

Bank/Co. Name: _____ Account Number: _____

K 401 Accounts:

Bank/Co. Name: _____ Account Number: _____

Bank/Co. Name: _____ Account Number: _____

Social Security Accounts: _____

INSURANCE POLICIES:

Co. Name: _____ Account Number: _____

Co. Name: _____ Account Number: _____

Co. Name: _____ Account Number: _____

REAL ESTATE:

_____

_____

POSSESSIONS:

_____

_____

DEBTS (such as credit cards, bank loans, etc.):

Bank/Co. Name: _____ Account Number: _____

Bank/Co. Name: _____ Account Number: _____

Bank/Co. Name: _____ Account Number: _____

Bank/Co. Name: _____ Account Number: _____

Chapter Three

The Nuts and Bolts of Financial Planning

Everyone who is caring for, or has cared for elderly parents knows it is not an easy job. You encounter difficulties you never imagined, hit bumps you never knew were there, and tread carefully around all sorts of sensitive issues. You're forced to deal with health issues, financial issues, housing issues, and even practical matters such as who will take Mom and Dad's trash to the curb for pick-up, or how Dad will get to his eye doctor's appointment now that he no longer can drive himself.

In Chapter Two, we discussed how important it is to learn all you can about your parents' financial situation, and how helping them to plan financially can save everyone a lot of anxiety and woe down the road. And, we talked about the importance of gathering all relevant information so that you're prepared if a situation occurs in which you need to begin handling your parents' finances.

In this chapter, we'll discuss the basics of financial planning, including how you can help your parents protect their assets and think about some basic estate planning. In order for you to help them, you've got to understand the issues.

Many people avoid talking to their parents about wills, estate planning, and related matters because they don't want to appear pushy or greedy. They're afraid that displaying any interest in these topics will appear as a desire to get their hands on Mom and Dad's money. And yet, many of our parents have failed to address these issues themselves.

If your parents have saved, invested, and planned for their estate, consider yourself very fortunate. Surveys show the majority of older Americans have not adequately planned to protect their assets and transfer property to heirs at the time of their deaths. This can happen for various reasons.

If people don't have substantial investments and bank accounts, and don't own property, they may feel as though they don't have enough wealth to make estate planning worthwhile. Or, one spouse may assume that he or she will die before the other, and the remaining spouse will take care of matters.

Many people, however, avoid estate planning, wills, trusts, and related matters because they simply don't care to address them. Some good friends—two sisters—are in the process of trying to get a handle on their elderly parent's financial situation, as well as their wishes concerning health care, funerals, and so forth. They're finding it to be extremely difficult. Pam, the younger sister, has in the past five years or so cared for both of her husband's parents as first one, and then the other, developed cancer and eventually died. She managed their finances, took care of household matters such as bill paying, cared for them while they were sick, took part in planning for their funerals, and helped to dispose of their property. She knows first-hand the importance of fully understanding an elderly parent's wishes and having full access to information and documents.

The older sister, Patrice, worries that her parents may soon need help managing their finances. She has overheard some discussions that indicate they don't fully understand some issues concerning their finances, and is afraid they'll start making mistakes and get into financial difficulty.

She also has tried to talk to her parents about their wishes for burial because they moved after retirement and no longer live in the area of their family cemetery. Patrice rightly feels it would be better to have this information now, than to have to deal with it after one of her parents has died. She wants to know if they have a will, and if so, how she can get a copy of it.

Pam and Patrice are in a very difficult position, however, because their parents refuse to talk about these matters. Their father has nothing to say about any such matters, and their mother, when questioned, becomes very flustered and irritated, and ends up giving them no information. The sisters discuss the matter frequently, but are at a loss about how to handle the situation.

Hopefully, if you're in a situation similar to the one facing Pam and Patrice, or you simply haven't addressed financial matters with your parents because you don't fully understand them, this chapter will help you to be able to sit down and talk intelligently and reasonably with Mom and Dad.

Financial Basics

Your parents may have little in the way of assets, or they could be quite well off, financially. You learned in Chapter Two how to get a handle on their net worth, so you should have an idea of the total of their assets.

Whether those assets total $100,000, $500,000, or $5 million, for you to help your folks manage their finances and plan their estate, you'll need to understand some financial basics as they apply to aging parents.

Remember that estate planning, asset management, and related topics can be quite complicated. You should consult a lawyer who understands the laws concerning these issues in your parents' state for help.

Let's start by considering investing and banking, as it may relate to older persons.

Investing and Banking

Over the years, your parents may have invested money in a variety of accounts. Many people have been investing in the stock and bond markets for many years, and have greatly increased their personal wealth. Hopefully, your parents' investments are diversified and have done well over the years. However, many people are extremely wary of the stock and bond markets, usually because they have little or no understanding of how they work.

While most people think that having investments is good, the act of investing in anything other than a standard bank account is very intimidating to many. As a result, many people fall into the keep-it-in-the-bank trap, stashing all their money into low-interest bank accounts. This can happen when someone doesn't know about or understand the many investment opportunities available, or when a person is mistrustful of other forms of investments.

Let's have a look at some common forms of investments in which your parents may be participating. As you know, the value of many investments fluctuate depending on market conditions and the state of the economy.

- **Mutual funds.** These are investments that pool the money of many people and place the cash into stocks, bonds, and other holdings. The pool of money, which may total hundreds of millions of dollars, is managed by a portfolio manager. Mutual funds are the most common investment vehicle for individuals. They're very popular because you don't need a lot of money to begin investing, and they offer opportunity for diversification. No-load mutual funds are those that let you avoid paying a sales commission on your transactions. You can get recommendations on which funds to buy from the companies that offer no-loads by phoning a toll-free number. You don't, however, work with an advisor or broker. If you buy load funds, you do work with a financial advisor, and you pay a sales commission. Some people are comfortable selecting their own mutual funds, while others like the security of working with an expert.

- **Money Markets.** There are two kinds of money markets: money market accounts and money market funds A money market account is a type of savings account, which generally pays a bit more interest than regular savings account and allows you to write a couple of checks on the account each month. These accounts are held with banks, and they're covered by the FDIC, the federal agency that insures the money in a bank. A money market fund is a type of mutual fund with a nonfluctuating $1 investment value per share. Like a savings account, if you put $1,000 into a money market fund, you'll get $1,000—plus interest—back out. Money market funds, which offer competitive interest rates and allow you to write checks on the account, are held within mutual fund companies. They're not federally insured. Generally, however, these funds are considered to be reasonably safe investments. Money market funds can offer some tax advantages, as well. Some types are called tax-free funds, and can get you some breaks on your federal, state, or local income tax.
- **Certificates of deposit.** These are investments that require you to deposit your money for a certain amount of time. The financial institution that holds the certificate of deposit agrees to pay you a certain interest rate and yield for the time that it has your money. Normally, the longer you keep your money in a certificate of deposit, the higher interest rate you'll get. If you withdraw your money before the specified amount of time has expired, you're penalized. Certificates of deposit generally pay more interest than savings or money market accounts. Most of them require a minimum amount to open, and banks or other financial institutions sometimes run "specials," during which they raise the interest rates they'll pay on certificates of deposit.
- **401(k)s.** If you parent has retired in the not-too-distant past, ask if he or she may have invested in a 401(k) retirement plan. Introduced in 1982 as an alternative to traditional pension plans, a 401(k) allows employees to contribute a portion of the paychecks to a company

investment plan. The employee gets to decide where his money should be invested by choosing from a list of various investment options provided by his employer through the plan. At retirement time, the money can either be left where it is, rolled over into another retirement account, or claimed by the individual. Many employers match a portion of their employees' contributions, making 401(k)s especially desirable—and lucrative.

- **Stocks.** Stocks are investments that represent ownership in a company. Companies—both large and small—sell stock in order to raise money. When you buy shares of stock, you're actually buying little pieces of the company. When the company makes a lot of money, the value of the stock increases, as does the value of your investment. If the company loses money, the value of its stock—and your investment—decrease. The more shares of stock in one company that you have, the bigger piece of the company you own. Owning shares of stock in a company makes you a shareholder of that company. There are different kinds of stocks, and some are riskier to own than others. If Mom owns a significant amount of stocks, now's the time to take a good look at her investments, anticipate her needs for the future, and perhaps unload high-risk stock. She may even consider selling some of her stock for income tax purposes.

- **Bonds.** Bonds are a type of lending investment. You loan your money with the understanding that you'll get it back—along with interest—after a specified period of time. The U.S. government issues bonds. So do state, municipal, and county governments. Some corporations offer bonds, along with hospitals, colleges, and government agencies. U.S. government bonds are backed by the federal government, and most bonds are considered to be fairly low-risk investments.

If Mom is still keeping all her money in a savings account, try to get her to consider looking at some other types of investments. It may be worth it for her to hire a good financial advisor. At this stage of her life, Mom needs to calculate her future cash needs, and make sure she has money that she can get to when she wants it. She shouldn't have all her funds tied up in an account she can't easily access, or in which she'll have to pay a penalty to get her money. She also should be sure that all IRAs, pension plans, and insurance policies are updated and current, with the proper beneficiary designations.

Insurance Policies

There are hundreds of types of insurance policies, available to protect everything from a fur coat against theft to a wedding day against rain. Insurance is a huge industry in this country, commanding a hefty chunk of our nation's economy. There are tens of thousands of insurance companies in the United States, employing more than one and a half million people.

It's estimated by the National Insurance Consumers Organization that one out of every 12 dollars American spend is to pay for some kind of insurance.

Insurance generally is sold through agents or brokers, who work for insurance companies such as Allstate, State Farm, Nationwide, Liberty Mutual, and thousands of others. The agents earn commission from the company for which they work, based on how much and what type of insurance they sell.

Let's have a look at some of the policies your parents are likely to own.

- **Health Insurance.** If your folks are 65 years or older, they're probably covered by Medicare, a health insurance program administered by the Centers for Medicare and Medicaid Service. Low-income seniors may be covered by Medicaid, which is a state-administered, but funded by state and federal governments, program. They may also have supplemental health care policies. You'll learn all about health care for seniors in Chapter Five.
- **Life insurance.** Many older people own life insurance policies, just because they bought them when they were younger and raising families and never got rid of them. Life insurance is necessary if you're supporting a family and that support will discontinue if you die. Elderly people who are no longer supporting families may no longer need life insurance, although many opt to keep it. The proceeds of their policies provide liquidity at their death for final expenses, burial costs, death taxes, and spending money for a surviving spouse. Basically there are two types of life insurance—term and cash value. Term life insurance pays a predetermined amount of money to your beneficiaries if you die during the term in which you're insured. All you have to do, of course, is keep paying your annual premium. The trick is, that the premium increases as you get older, and may eventually become prohibitive. Most

people can't afford to keep the coverage as they get older because the cost increases so much.

Under a cash value life insurance plan, on the other hand, part of the premium is used to provide death benefits, and the rest is used to earn interest or be invested within mutual funds, depending on the type of policy. It's both a protection plan and a savings plan that can actually provide some income in your later years. If your parent still has life insurance, it's likely to be a cash value plan. One type of cash value insurance invests your money in an assortment of mutual funds, while the other invests it in something similar to a certificate of deposit, with a fixed interest rate.

- **Homeowner's insurance.** If your parent owns a home, he'll need homeowner's insurance to cover the structure and contents. Property, or homeowner's insurance protects you from what the insurance industry calls "perils." Perils include damage from: fire, lightning, smoke, aircraft, rioting, vehicles, vandalism, an explosion, wind, hail, and hurricanes. Broken glass, property loss and theft also are considered to be perils. Property insurance varies greatly, so it's a good idea to check out your folks' policy to see what it covers. Make sure that the policy covers not only damage to the structure, but to the contents, as well. Personal property coverage usually insures belongings up to 50 percent of the coverage on the structure. You should check to make sure your parents have enough coverage to protect the complete set of sterling silver handed down from Great-Great-Grandma, or Dad's collection of rare coins. Riders can be attached to a homeowner's policy to provide additional coverage.

- **Auto insurance.** Some elderly people have great difficulty with auto insurance because their carrier will drop them if they file any sort of claim, or even have any traffic violations. Many companies require seniors to pay higher rates than a younger person. Everyone needs auto insurance, because the liability risk if you're in an accident is too great to ignore. In addition, most states require it. Auto insurance includes different types of coverage, but the one that nearly all states require is liability. Liability covers bodily injury and property damage for you and others, if you're at fault in an accident. Most states require that you carry a minimum amount of bodily injury coverage—usually $25,000 per person, and $50,000 per accident.

- **Personal catastrophic casualty insurance (PCAT).** Auto and home-owner's policies provide liability coverage up to a certain amount, but people with sizeable assets should consider personal catastrophic casualty insurance. This protects them if someone sues for more than the limitations of their existing policies. A PCAT policy comes in $1 million increments. A PCAT policy supplements other policies, and is not overly expensive (usually about $150 a year). Such a policy should cover damages from home accidents and automobile accidents.
- **Disability insurance.** You can't get this type of insurance if you're not working, so if Mom and Dad are retired, you can skip over this section. If they are working, they may have disability insurance through their employers. Disability insurance kicks in when a working person is unable to do his job because of a physical or mental disability. It is to protect a person who depends on a salary for income.

Your parents may well have other types of policies, as well. If they—or you—aren't sure they have the policies they need for the amounts they need, it would be a good idea to talk to an insurance agent.

Safe-Deposit Boxes

People have been storing their valuables in safe-deposit boxes for more than 100 years, and it's likely that your parents are doing the same. Located within banks, safe-deposit boxes are used to store personal property that is important or expensive, and difficult or impossible to replace. Many people use the boxes to store insurance policies, stock certificates, jewelry, birth certificates, property records, business contracts, adoption papers, will, inventories of household valuables, and so forth.

If your parent has a safe-deposit box, she pays a small rental fee, and has access to the box during bank hours. Generally, two keys are needed to open the box. Mom will have one, and the bank keeps the other. If your parents have their wills in their safe-deposit box, make sure that either you, another family member, or their lawyer, has a copy, as well.

Talk to your folks about their safe deposit box, and suggest that they authorize you, or another family member, as their agent. Because banks are responsible for preventing anyone other than the customer from gaining access to the box, so you won't be able to open it without your parent's advance permission, even if you have the key. Some states require that safe-deposit boxes be sealed when the person renting the box dies.

Make sure that you know in which bank the box is located, the number of the box, and where the key is stored. If your parent dies without having appointed you as agent, ask the bank to provide access to the box to check for a will. Bank personnel probably will be willing to do that, but you shouldn't be permitted to take anything else from the box at that time. Your parent's appointed executor or administrator can open the box at a later time.

Understanding Power of Attorney

When your dad gets tired of mowing the lawn and trimming the hedges, he gets the kid down the street to come and take care of it. When he feels he can no longer climb up on his extension ladder to paint the trim around the second-story windows, he hires somebody to do it. Your mother has no qualms in admitting that the housework is getting the best of her and hiring someone to help her with the cleaning.

Your parents may seem to be a lot more sensitive, though, when you suggest they appoint someone to help them manage their finances. While perfectly willing to relinquish control of household chores, they cling to their control over their business affairs.

This is perfectly normal and understandable. And, as you've already read in previous chapters, talking with your parents about appointing someone to help them with financial matters probably will not be easy. A woman who is a retirement planning specialist and vice president of a major financial firm said she was shocked at how difficult it was for her to ask her father to appoint her as his agent via the power of attorney. Although she counsels all her older clients to sign powers of attorney, and her younger ones to address the matter with their parents, she had an extremely difficult time talking about power of attorney with her own parents.

"It was incredibly difficult," she said. "I couldn't imagine that it would have been such an emotional thing, but it was."

If you've noticed that Dad's becoming less and less able to handle his financial affairs, however, it's probably time to suggest he appoint an agent in a power of attorney. And, the time to do this is before the situation is out of control. A person must be competent in order to set up a power of attorney. If there's already a question about Dad's competency, you should get a doctor's certification, so you can be assured the power of attorney will be valid.

The person who executes a power of attorney is called the principal. The person authorized to act legally on behalf of the principal is called the agent, or attorney-in-fact.

A power of attorney is simply a document in which Dad authorizes another person to act legally on his behalf. The person whom Dad names is called the agent, or attorney-in-fact, although he or she certainly doesn't need to be a lawyer. Any trusted person—a spouse, child, other relative, or friend—can serve as attorney-in-fact. It should, however, be someone who will be sensitive to Dad's wishes and with whom Dad is very comfortable.

The agent is able to handle chores like writing checks, buying or selling property, investing savings, and entering into contracts. The agent has the legal power to act on behalf of the other person for any and all powers given.

As pointed out in Chapter Two, signing a power of attorney doesn't mean that Dad immediately gives up all control of his finances and business matters. He can make it clear that he intends to see to his own finances for as long as he's able to do so, and the job of the agent is simply to help when necessary.

All Power of Attorney is Not the Same

When addressing the issue of power of attorney, it's important for you and your parent or parents to understand that there are different types of documents.

- A general power of attorney, or simple power of attorney, remains in effect until the time that the principal should become incompetent. When a doctor declares the agent to be incompetent, a general power of attorney becomes invalid.
- A durable power of attorney, on the other hand, remains in effect even after the principal has been medically determined to be incompetent. It's a better document, because it remains valid during the time your parent can no longer make decisions on his own, and is most in need of your help.
- A medical power of attorney is a document that allows an individual to appoint someone else to make decisions about his medical care if he's unable to communicate. You'll learn a lot more about medical power of attorney in Chapter Four.
- A limited power of attorney is one executed for a particular reason. It may specify that the agent may write checks and handle all day-to-day finan-

cial matters, but not enter into contracts or buy or sell property on behalf of the principal.

- A lesser-known type of document is a springing power of attorney. This document becomes valid only when the principal is declared to be mentally incompetent. When a doctor certifies that Dad has lost capacity, a springing power of attorney goes into effect.

Advantages and Disadvantages of Power of Attorney

Appointing an agent in a durable power of attorney is relatively easy and inexpensive. There are pre-printed forms available, but it's probably a good idea to have a lawyer draft a power of attorney so you and your parents can make sure it contains exactly what you wish.

While many people set up joint bank accounts as a means of allowing one person to handle financial matters for another, a durable power of attorney authorizes the agent to act legally on behalf of the principal, it does not give the agent access to the principal's money for his own use. A power of attorney authorizes the agent only to use the principal's assets on behalf of the principal.

Executing a power of attorney can provide significant peace of mind, if it's done before the situation is out of control. If Dad is having a lot of trouble managing his finances, for instance, and Mom has never written a check in her life, appointing an agent can give them both assurance that matters will be taken care of.

The main potential disadvantage of a durable power of attorney is that it doesn't require much accountability, and therefore can be subject to abuse. Even though the principal's assets can only be used to his or her advantage, an agent could act in other ways on his own behalf, such as entering into a contract from which he could benefit.

Guardianship

As you've just learned, a durable power of attorney can only be executed while the principal is mentally competent to do so. If your parent has already progressed to the point where he or she is incompetent, your situation, unfortunately, becomes more difficult.

In order to gain control of your parent's affairs without a durable power of attorney, you'll need to be appointed guardian by the court. This is much more expensive than having a durable power of attorney already in place, and it's an extreme measure that removes all of the legal rights of your parent.

You'll need a lawyer to petition the court, after which the court will appoint a lawyer to represent your parent. There will be a hearing, during which people involved with your parent's care, such as a doctor or visiting nurse, may be interviewed. Your parent will be notified by the court of the hearing, and can attend if he wishes.

If guardianship is granted and your parent declared incompetent, he loses his legal right to vote, drive a car, sell or buy property, handle his finances, enter into any type of contract, or have any say concerning his own medical care or living arrangements.

As you can see, seeking guardianship is not something you'd want to do unless it is absolutely necessary. The matter requires a great deal of careful consideration. The expense, emotional upheaval, inevitable delay in the decision-making process, and the need for continual court approval on many decisions make a guardianship a definite last resort.

Protecting Their Assets While Your Parents are Alive

A primary goal of most people is to protect the assets they have. Regardless of whether they'll have anything left to pass along to their children and grandchildren, your parents certainly want to make sure they protect the assets they have. No one likes to think about being a burden to her children, or not having enough money with which to live comfortably. The best thing you can do for your parents is to help them think about protecting their assets before their situation reaches a critical point.

If you see that Mom is getting to the point where she'll soon need to be in a nursing home, you'll probably be worried not only about her health and the emotional aspects of sending her to a home, but the financial aspects, as well. If Dad is still alive and wants to remain at home, you've got to know how to protect his assets so that he can continue to live comfortably.

It used to be that married couples would have to spend nearly all their money in order for a spouse to qualify for Medicaid, which is a government-funded assistance program for low-income seniors. Medicaid, unlike Medicare, pays for nursing home care where it's available. Medicare rules have changed, however, to include "spousal impoverishment" provisions. These provisions allow Dad to hang on to some of his assets while Mom is in the nursing home.

If Mom goes into the nursing home, and it's clear that she'll be there for at least 30 days, your parents can request what's called a "resource assessment." To do this, they must submit a form to their county assistance office, on which they'll list all their assets as of the date Mom entered the home. Certain assets, including the couple's home and household goods, do not have to be included on the list of assets. Some states allow Dad to exclude his IRAs, as well.

Once the list of assets has been evaluated, Dad will be notified of his spousal share, which determines the amount of assets he gets to keep. Basically, his share will be a half of all the assets that were listed on the form, plus he still has the house, household goods, his personal belongings, and IRAs. If the amount of assets totaled $150,000, Dad gets to keep $75,000 in assets, while Mom's share will go toward paying the nursing home bill or other expenses until she becomes eligible for medical assistance.

There are limits on this spousal share, which may vary from state to state. In Pennsylvania in 2001, the minimum share Dad would receive would be $17,400, even if the total assets were not valued at twice that amount. On the other hand, if total assets add up to $200,000 or more, Dad gets to keep just $87,000—not half of the total amount. Dad also may be entitled to a maintenance allowance.

The situation becomes more grim if Mom or Dad is single, or if both parents require nursing home care. A single person can have only very limited assets (it varies from state to state, but is normally somewhere around $2,500) to be eligible for medical assistance. Some possessions, including an automobile, household goods and personal effects, small life insurance policies, and small amounts saved for burial expenses, are not included when tallying assets. In some cases, but not all, a single person's home may be excluded.

Anticipating the future need for nursing home care, some people "spend down" their money so that they're eligible for medical assistance by the time the need to go to the home. Perhaps your parents have worked very hard all their lives with the hope of leaving something behind for you and your siblings. Or, maybe the farm has been in Dad's family for six generations, and he wants more than anything to be able to pass it along to a child or grandchild. Looking ahead and seeing the need for nursing home care, they might decide to dispose of some of their assets now, rather than having them go to pay for their care.

They do this by transferring property, gifting money, setting up trusts, and so forth. Dad might decide to put the deed of the farm in his grandson's name now in order to be assured that it will stay in the family. While he'd be allowed to keep the property until his death, the state would claim anything remaining in his estate in order to repay its costs for Dad's nursing care. Changing the deed to his grandson's name allows Dad to remove the farm from the reach of state officials and other creditors at the time of his death.

Be aware, however, that there are many restrictions in place to discourage this practice. And, many people have ethical problems with spending down in order to get public money. You'll read more about the restrictions in place in Chapter 5.

If you think you may be looking at nursing home situation for one of your parents, don't wait to start investigating methods of protecting their assets. Talk to an elder care attorney or financial planner who specializes in elderly issues.

Estate Planning

Estate planning is a huge topic, with entire books devoted to the topic. You can find the names of some good ones, in fact, by checking the additional resources appendix in the back of this book.

Estate planning helps to assure that a person's assets will be distributed in the manner he or she would like, and can help to reduce the amount of tax heirs will have to pay. Not only people with lots of assets benefit from estate planning, although it may be more important in order to protect those assets.

The federal so-called "death tax" laws have currently been revised. The rule of thumb for federal taxes kicking in are when a person's estate total more than a certain amount. An estate, by the way, is simply all of a person's property and possessions. In 2001, before death tax law revisions, death taxes didn't kick in until a person's estate was valued at more than $675,000. The figure rises to $1,000,000 in 2006. That is, all money over those amounts will be taxed. If the estate was valued at less than that amount, no federal taxes applied, although it may still have been subject to state taxes, for which the amount varies. The federal tax rate is based on the value of the estate, ranging from 37 to 50 percent.

In this section, you'll get some basic information about estate planning. We'll look at the very basic, and very important issues of wills, trusts, and gifting, as they apply to estate planning. You'll really need, however, to consult a financial planner or lawyer who specializes in estate planning for more information in order to fully help your parents.

Wills and Letters of Instruction

Everyone who is of legal age and has any assets at all should have a will, there's simply no question about it. If your parent, or you, for that matter, dies without a will, the court will determine how property is distributed and appoint someone to take charge of closing out the estate. The person or firm appointed can charge up to 5 percent of the value of the estate.

Most lawyers will draft a basic will for $250 or less. You can buy generic legal forms, including wills, but be aware that not all states accept generic documents, and these forms aren't customized, so they may not be exactly what your parent needs.

If both of your parents are alive, they should each have a will. If your parents or parent already has a will, make sure that it's updated, and find out if there are any codicils, which are amendments to the will. Let's take a look at what sort of information might be included in a will.

- Description of a person's assets, property, and belongings.
- Description of how those things are to be divided after the person's death.
- Specific instructions assigning certain items to individuals.
- The name or names of the person or people assigned as executors.

Many people include a letter of instruction along with their will to address more personal and specific issues. Some of those issues could include the following:

- Special instructions for the funeral or burial.
- Detailed lists of possessions to be passed along to various people.
- Locations of all important documents and items.
- Lists of all insurance policies, stocks, bank accounts, access numbers, and so forth.
- Personal messages to family members or friends.
- Instructions concerning debt or other matters.
- Help your parents to protect their assets by making sure they have valid, updated wills, letters of instructions, and any other pertinent documents.

Duties of an Executor

A will normally includes the name or names of a person or persons who will administer the estate. This person is called an executor, or an executrix, if it's a woman. While some people consider it an honor to be named as executor, others dread the thought of being responsible for so many details.

The executor of a will is responsible for paying any owed taxes or outstanding bills, and for seeing that the wishes of the decedent are carried out. He or she also is responsible for the following tasks:
- Identifying and listing all debt
- Notifying creditors that they need to file claims for payment
- Filing claims with insurance companies
- Inventorying all assets
- Arranging for appraisals of assets
- Closing bank and investment accounts of the decedent
- Setting up a checking account to use to pay bills
- Gathering and then distributing all assets according to the decedent's wishes
- Filing final income tax returns
- Filing the state and federal death tax returns, if applicable

An executor should be chosen carefully, with thought given to the time it will take. Your parent might consider, for instance, asking a sibling who does not work full time or whose children are grown to be executor, rather than a full-time working mom with three school-aged kids.

Executing a Will

In the movies, after someone dies, the family sits down with a lawyer who's always an old, trusted friend for a dramatic reading of the will. The will (in the movies, that is) normally contains some sort of shocking revelation, causing the parties present to burst into tears or storm off in anger.

In real life, it's normally not that dramatic. You don't need to be in the presence of a lawyer to read a will, and most people don't end up absolutely floored by its contents. You may, however, be in for a long wait until the will is executed and the estate of the deceased person is settled. If necessary, wills go through probate, which is the legal process involved. Probate can be a long, drawn-out process, sometimes lasting for years and costing thousands and thousands of dollars in legal fees.

Small estates may qualify for small estate administration, which is a simplified form (and much quicker) form of probate. Small estate administration is handled through a court order, and normally takes no more than a couple of months to be completed. Probate can get really complicated if the deceased person owned property in more than one state, requiring each state to participate in the process.

Many, if not most, wills stipulate that property should be equally divided between children, assuming that there is no spouse or partner to be considered. While this is no doubt a caring instruction on the part of the deceased, those words have caused big trouble in among thousands of siblings. Many families have been torn apart over the distribution of property during the settling of an estate. Suddenly, neither of two brothers can bear to live without Dad's baseball card collection that's been gathering dust in the attic for 15 years. Or, his college ring becomes a much-coveted and fought about commodity.

If you're in the position of dividing a parent's estate, try to keep matters in perspective. Do you really need the Wedgewood china? Could you live without the Waterford crystal, or Dad's tools, or the painting that hung over the fireplace?

Sure, it's nice to have objects that have some meaning and sentimental value. It's also nice to have some belongings that may be valuable. But, material possessions can never replace family relationships, especially after the death of a parent or parents. When you get right down to it, human relationships are by far the most valuable possessions we can have. So, be gentle when dividing that estate. Don't rush into it, if it can be helped, and don't try to clean out an entire house in a weekend. It probably took your parents 30, 40, or 50 years to accumulate all those belongings. There's no good reason to try to dispose of them all within two or three days.

Trusts

Many people set up trusts in order to manage their assets while they're living, and to transfer those assets at the time of their death. Trusts allow you to transfer ownership of property or money to a person who is designated to manage and distribute the assets according to your instructions. Some trusts may provide significant tax advantages. The person who establishes the trust is called the "grantor." The person who manages the trust is known as the "trustee," and the people who eventually receive money or other assets from a trust are called "beneficiaries."

There are many varieties of trusts, but all fall under three basic categories.

Testamentary Trust

This type of trust is laid out in a person's will and established after his death. The grantor keeps control of the assets included in the trust during his lifetime, and can stipulate when beneficiaries should receive their money or property from the trust. Testamentary trusts can help to reduce estate taxes.

Revocable Living Trust

This kind of trust is set up while the grantor is still living, and allows the grantor to keep full control of the assets. The grantor also has the ability to revoke or amend the terms of the trust, or change the appointed trustee.

A revocable living trust becomes irrevocable when the grantor dies or becomes incapacitated. Many people consider a revocable living trust to be a substitute for a will, because the trust instructs how assets should be distributed. It's extremely difficult, however, for a trust to include everything covered in a will. If your parent has a revocable living trust, she should still have a will.

A revocable living trust can reduce the cost of settling an estate, and also the amount of time it takes. It also can protect privacy because assets included in the trust don't have to pass through probate, which is a court in which a person's estate is settled. All creditors are paid off during probate, and heirs receive their shares of the estate. And, while wills can be contested, trusts cannot.

Irrevocable Trust

Usually set up and used by people with many assets, irrevocable trusts, as the name implies, can't be amended or destroyed. Once the trust is set up, it remains in place, giving the grantor no opportunity to change his mind.

Irrevocable trusts are used primarily to reduce estate taxes. When a person turns over property to the trust, she no longer owns the property if she is not a beneficiary of the trust. If she does not own the property placed in the trust, it can't be considered as part of the estate. That property may still be subject to other taxes, such gift or capital gains, but those traditionally have been far lower than estate taxes.

They also can be used to protect property for minor heirs, or those otherwise unable to be responsible for their inheritance. Irrevocable trusts also can be used to channel income to a secondary beneficiary when a primary beneficiary dies.

As with a revocable living trust, assets included in an irrevocable trust do not have to pass through probate. They are interesting estate planning tools, but you and your parents should speak with an attorney and other advisors to see if an irrevocable trust makes sense for your family's situation.

Gifting

If you're lucky enough that the amount of your parents' estate is large enough that they're looking for ways to reduce it, or if circumstances are forcing you and a parent to look at ways to quickly reduce the value of an estate, you might suggest gifting.

An individual can give $10,000 per year to as many people as he or she wants, and nobody has to pay taxes on any of it. If Mom and Dad have the means, they can give $10,000 a year to you, your spouse, your kids, and all your siblings and their kids, and nobody pays a dime in taxes. Not many people, of course, are able to dole out $10,000 each year to each member of the family, but gifting is a good means of reducing the value of an estate. Experts often recommend gifting if a person has learned that he or she has a terminal illness and will not live much longer. You'll read more about financial planning for a terminally ill parent in Chapter Four. If you're lucky enough that the amount of your parents' estate is large enough that they're looking for ways to reduce it, you might suggest gifting.

Tax-free gifts in addition to a $10,000 gift may be given if the money is paid directly to an institution for medical costs or education. If Mom wants to, for instance, she can send money to her grandson's college to pay for his tuition, and she won't be subject to gift tax on that money. That can happen even if she's already given the grandson $10,000 that year.

There is a catch to gifting, as you might have imagined. The total of gifts given is subtracted from the amount at which estate taxes kick in (called the exemption amount). That means, if your parent gives away $100,000 in gifts, her estate will be taxed at anything over $910,000 instead of the usual $1,000,000. And, gifts of over $10,000 are subject to a federal gift tax that mirrors the estate tax. This gift tax, however, isn't due until the amount of all gifting is greater than the federal estate exemption amount. Gifting can be a great estate planning tool, but it's a complicated matter. Again, it's a good idea to meet with a financial advisor before taking action.

If this little bit of information on estate planning has given you the impression that it's not simple, nor something you should undertake on your own, you've read it correctly. People devote entire careers to becoming experts on estate planning, and, if your parents have any notable assets, it will be worth your time to consult one of them.

A Glossary of Terms Found in Chapter Three

bond A type of lending instrument in which you loan your money with the understanding that you'll get it back—plus interest—after a specified period of time.

cash value life insurance plan A type of life insurance in which part of the premium is used to provide death benefits, while the rest earns interest or is invested within mutual funds.

certificate of deposit A receipt for a deposit of funds in a financial institution that permits the holder to receive interest plus the deposit at maturity.

codicil A legally recognized change or amendment to a will.

executor A person appointed in a will to administer the estate of a person who dies.

401(k) plan A retirement plan valued for its tax advantages in which you can contribute a portion of your currently salary.

estate planning A type of financial planning that utilizes many avenues and is intended to maximize assets and minimize taxes paid at the time of a person's death.

gifting A means of shrinking an estate for tax purposes, in which an individual can give up to $10,000 a year to as many people as desired without any tax consequences.

guardianship The legal process of having a person declared incompetent and a legal guardian appointed to make decisions and take control of financial and legal matters.

insurance A mechanism that permits individuals to reduce risk by sharing the losses associated with the occurrence of uncertain events, such as sickness, death, theft, etc.

investment The process of purchasing securities or property for which stability of value and level of expected returns are somewhat predictable.

Medicaid A state-administered health insurance program for people with limited incomes. Medicaid is funded by state and federal governments.

Medicare A health insurance program for elderly or disabled persons, administered by the Centers for Medicare and Medicaid Service.

money market account A type of savings account, held within a bank, which generally pays a bit more interest than regular savings account and allows you to write a couple of checks on the account each month.

money market fund A type of mutual fund that sells shares of ownership and uses the proceeds to buy short-term, high-qualities securities. Income received by shareholders is in the form of additional stocks. Money market funds have a non-fluctuating $1 investment value per share.

mutual fund An open-end investment company that invests its shareholders' money in a diversified group of securities and other corporations. Mutual funds usually are diversified and professionally managed.

personal catastrophic casualty insurance (PCAT) A type of insurance policy, sold in $1 million increments, that protects the insured if someone sues for more than the limitations of existing policies.

power of attorney A legal document in which one person authorizes another person to act legally on his behalf. The person who executes the power of attorney is called the principal, while the person appointed to act on his behalf is the agent. There are different types of powers of attorney.

safe deposit box A storage area located within a bank for which clients pay a fee to keep valuables such as wills and other legal documents, jewelry, and so forth.

stock Shares of ownership in a company that increase or decrease in value depending on the profitability of the company.

term life insurance A type of life insurance that pays a predetermined amount of money to beneficiaries if the insured dies during the term in which he's covered. The premium generally increases as the insured gets older.

trust A method of holding money, property, or other assets. There are many types of trusts, established for all kinds of reasons. Many trusts are set up as part of estate planning.

Chapter Four

Planning for Your Parents' Health Needs

Although helping your parents to plan financially is an extremely important task, it is by no means the only job associated with care giving. Planning for and tending to the health needs of your parents is another chore for which you may be summoned. If so, you should know that working within the health care system is likely to be just as complicated, if not more so, as managing your parents' financial matters.

Regulations concerning health care issues tend to change as often as a teenager dressing for a dance. The health care system can be pretty intimidating to the uninitiated, and it's a lot better to have an idea of how it works ahead of time than to be thrown into it without any warning or preparation.

Imagine that you come home from shopping at the mall with your daughter one day, and your husband tells you that your mother called a couple of hours ago. Your father has had a heart attack and is admitted to his local hospital, about an hour away from your house. By the time you drive to the hospital, he's had another heart attack, and has been taken by helicopter to a university hospital in a large city that's an additional hour of driving. You find your mother sitting in the hospital's lobby and you suspect she's in a state of shock. You finally find your father's doctor, who tells you that Dad's condition is very critical, and, even though performing immediate heart surgery will be very risky, his chances of survival without it are extremely slim.

Without warning, your life completely changes. You and your mother rush to the city hospital where your dad's being prepared for surgery. You call your sister and brother, who live in different states, and tell them to get there as soon as possible. The doctor asks if your father has a living will or a durable health care power of attorney, and advises you to get copies of them. The next few days become a blur as you sit in the hospital—waiting, hoping, and praying. You drive home to change clothes and—finally—to get some sleep. The next day, and every day afterward for six long weeks as your father struggles to recover in the hospital, you juggle your job, your family, and your home with two-hour trips back and forth to visit him. You're worried sick about your father, and nearly as worried about Mom. You know she's not eating or sleeping much, and she's wearing herself out trying to keep up with all the household chores your that she and your dad did together.

In the midst of this emotional turmoil, you're getting an unsolicited crash course on the ins and outs of the health care system. You meet with doctors on a regular basis, and are even starting to understand their medical jargon. When doctors aren't available, you talk with nurses about your father's condition. You meet with therapists, patient advocates, and social workers. You learn about more types of drugs than you ever thought existed. You don't understand why they've changed your father's room three times, and you can't find anyone who can tell you. You sit up until after midnight, trying to figure out the stack of insurance statements that have piled up on your desk. You try to make sense out of what almost looks to be another language: HMOs, Medi-gap, Medicare. You meet with siblings to figure out how you'll share the care giving responsibilities that are sure to come. You debate whether Dad will need to go to a nursing home. You schedule an appointment for your mother with her doctor because you're worrying more and more about her health. Her visit results in more insurance forms.

Dealing with a traumatic experience such as that described above is never easy. But, having an idea of your parents' wishes concerning their health care, and a basic understanding of how the health care system operates can make such an experience easier to deal with. In this chapter, we'll discuss many aspects of that system, as well as topics such as long-term health care insurance and prescription medicines.

Health Care and Financial Planning Go Hand in Hand

Although they may appear to be two different topics, you really can't separate health care and financial planning. Each is directly related and dependent on the other. Medical bills incurred due to poor health will impact directly on your parents' finances. And, both short-term and possible long-term health needs must be considered when you're trying to plan your parents' financial future. Should money be put aside in case nursing home care becomes necessary? How much out-of-pocket should you figure each month for prescription medicines? Should you look into long-term health care insurance, even though it's expensive?

None of us like to think about our parents' deaths. And, to many people, financial planning with an eye to a parent's health and life expectancy seems somehow insensitive or even disrespectful. It would be extremely difficult for most people to suggest to an extremely ill parent that he or she considers giving money away now in order to avoid extra taxes after death. Or, conversely, to tell a healthy parent with a long life expectancy that he or she is not going to be able to afford to stay in the family home because the expenses are too high.

Most of this chapter deals with issues relating to health care, such as living wills, advance directives, and the high cost of prescription medicine. For now, however, let's just take a few minutes to look at how financial planning considerations vary, depending on the health and life expectancy of your parent.

Planning for the Long—or Short Term

Hopefully, your parents are well, and will live for many more years. If this is the case, however, you'll need to pay attention to some particular issues when considering their financial plan.

Chapter Two covered many considerations of long-term planning, which may include controlling or reducing expenses, looking for additional means of income, reassessing insurance policies, examining medical costs, paying off high-interest debt, and so forth. And, while helping your parents plan financially for the next 15 or 20 years is no walk in the park, it's nothing compared to helping a parent who has a very short life expectancy.

If you've learned that your parent has been diagnosed with a terminal illness and given only a short time to live, or your parent is very ill and it's clear—even without a diagnosis—that he or she will not live much longer, you'll need to make some difficult decisions concerning the financial situation.

You can avoid any mention of finances and concentrate on making your parent's last days as pleasant and comfortable as possible. Or, if your parent has not done sufficient estate planning, you may want to help her, assuming she's willing, take steps to provide some financial advantages to those who will inherit her estate.

As you can imagine, many people are unable emotionally to talk about finances with a dying parent. And, many people who are close to death may not be at all interested in financial matters, or may be physically or mentally incapable of doing so. If that's the case, don't beat yourself up over it. Do, however, consider the importance of planning financially before it's too late.

You read about estate planning in Chapter Three. Experts, however, suggest certain strategies in particular if it is clear that the person planning the estate does not have much longer to live. Those strategies include:

- Gifting. If it's clear that your mother will not need her money to live on, she might want to reduce her estate by gifting. If you remember from Chapter Three, Mom can give gifts of up to $10,000 to as many people as wants to without tax consequences to her or the recipient. She may also want to give away expensive jewelry or other items in order to reduce the value of the estate.
- Consider her bank accounts. If Mom's name is the only one on her bank accounts, she may want to consider adding yours, or another family member's, at this point. This makes it easier to dispose of the accounts, or to use them to pay off debts after death.
- Take a look at the safe-deposit box. Some states require that safe-deposit boxes be sealed at the time of death, which can make it difficult to access their contents. You might want to find out what's in the safe-deposit box, and consider whether there's any reason to remove any items.
- Pre-pay funeral expenses, using your parent's money. As grisly as it sounds, it's better financial planning for your parent to pre-pay her funeral expenses, than for you to have to pay for them after death. Even if you'll receive assets from your mother's estate, that probably won't occur until a significant amount of time after her death. If you don't have the money to pay for the type of funeral your mother wants, or you want for her, it's smarter to pre-pay costs.
- Pay down debt, or better yet, eliminate it. While there may be plenty of money in Mom's estate to pay off any debt she might have, it's smarter to eliminate as much of it as possible before her death. This avoids the possibility of red tape or complications that could delay payment.

Coping with the impending death of your parent is tremendously difficult, to be sure. Don't assume, however, that she won't want to deal with financial matters at this time. Many people are relieved to be able to sort out last bits of business and know that everything has been taken care of, rather than left for survivors to deal with.

Regardless of your parents' current health situation, if you're helping them with their financial matters, remember to keep an eye turned to health care issues. The two definitely go hand in hand.

Knowing Your Parents' Wishes Concerning Health-Related Issues

It's difficult to talk to someone you love about tough issues such as how they feel about being kept alive on life support, or whether they would consider donating their organs after death. And yet, it's far better to understand your parents' wishes regarding their health care before they get sick, than to try to guess what they might want when they're not able to tell you.

So, take a deep breath and tell yourself that you can do this. You can sit down with Mom and Dad and ask them not only what kind of insurance they have and the names of all their doctors, but whether they would want their lives prolonged by medical measures if their conditions were terminal and death certain. Try to be reassuring and positive. Tell them that knowing their wishes will make it much easier for you to act as their advocate in the event that they're sick. Let them know that you have their best interests in mind, but in order to be able to help, you've got to know what they want. Urge them to write those wishes down in a legal document that you can access if it becomes necessary.

We're fortunate to live in a country in which we have choices regarding our health care. Unfortunately, many people do not realize they have a choice. Congress in 1991 enacted legislation called the Patient Self-Determination Act. This act requires any facility that administers health care (hospitals, nursing homes, home health agencies, rehabilitation centers, and so forth) to tell patients they have the right to either accept or reject medical care. Nearly every medical facility receives some federal aid, so they all should be letting patients know about this option. Some, however, do not bother to do so, and many patients don't realize they have the right to say "no thanks" to a particular medical procedure. Federally funded facilities also are required by law to release information concerning advance directives and their particular state's regulations concerning them. Again, however, some facilities don't bother to do this.

Your parents may have strong beliefs and wishes concerning the care they'll receive if they should become ill, especially if they're not capable of expressing their wishes. It's your job to find out how they feel so that you can act as an advocate when necessary.

Advance Directives

Advance directives are legal documents that state specific instructions for medical care in the event that one becomes seriously ill or incapacitated, and unable to make his own medical decisions. There are two kinds of advance directives: living wills and medical powers of attorney.

Advance directives are legally recognized in every state in the United States, but are regulated differently from state to state. Your parent's lawyer will be able to help them to draft a living will or medical power of attorney. Or, an organization called Partnership for Caring, Inc.—formerly known as Choice in Dying, Inc.— provides living will and medical power of attorney forms that comply with the regulations of each state. To get forms that are specific to your state, you can contact the agency at 475 Riverside Drive, Suite 1825, New York, NY 10115. The phone number is 212-870-2003, and the fax number is 212-870-2040. Or, you can download the forms from Partnership for Caring's web site at www.partnershipforcaring.org.

Another organization, Aging With Dignity, offers a form called "Five Wishes," which serves as both a living will and a medial power of attorney. It's legally in valid in 35 states and the District of Columbia. You can order "Five Wishes" on line at www.agingwithdignity.org, or by calling or writing to Aging With Dignity. The address is P.O. Box 1661, Tallahassee, FL 32302-1661, and the phone number is 850-681-2010. The fax number is 850-681-2481.

Advance directives are useless if nobody knows that they exist or where to find them. If your parent has completed an advanced directive and it's properly witnessed and notarized if required, copies should be distributed to the appropriate people and places. These include:

- Family members
- Primary physician and specialists
- The person chosen to make medical decisions in the event your parent can not
- The hospital to which your parent would be taken if an emergency would occur

If Mom needs to go to a nursing home or assisted living facility, it also should get a copy of her advance directives. Don't assume, however, that because her directives have been distributed to the proper places and people that everyone will know that they're there and access them when necessary. Always remind her health care provider or other applicable person that the documents exist. Let's have a look at the differences between a living will and a medical power of attorney.

Living Wills

A living will states a person's preferences for medical treatment at the end of life. It is intended to be used when the person can no longer communicate or make decisions on her own, and is designed to guide family members and medical personnel regarding which medical treatment the patient wishes to have, and which she does not. A living will goes into effect when a doctor has determined that death is fairly certain, or when it's been determined that a person is permanently unconscious.

Living wills and medical powers of attorney are known by different names in some states. A living will also may be known as a directive to physicians, health care declaration, declaration with respect to life-sustaining treatment, or medical directive. A medical power of attorney may be referred to as a health care proxy, appointment of health care agent, or a durable health care power of attorney. If your parent wishes to draft a living will or medical power of attorney, be sure you use a form that's valid in your state.

A living will may start out something like this one, which was drafted by a lawyer in Pennsylvania:

I, Janet E. Jones, being of sound mind, willfully and voluntarily make this declaration to be followed if I become incompetent. This declaration reflects my firm and settled commitment to refuse life-sustaining treatment under the circumstances listed below.

The document goes on to direct the attending physicians to withhold or withdraw life-sustaining treatment that "serves only to prolong the process of my dying," in the event that the patient is in a terminal condition or a state of permanent unconsciousness. It instructs that the only treatment given should be with the purpose of keeping the patient comfortable and relieving pain.

This particular living will, as most, lists the patient's wishes regarding specific types of medical treatment. It instructs that the patient does not wish to have:
- Cardiac resuscitation
- Mechanical respiration
- Tube feeding or any other artificial or invasive form of food or water

- Blood or blood products
- Kidney dialysis
- Antibiotics

Some living wills also include directions about whether or not the patient should be taken to the hospital, and include specific instructions to ensure that the patient is kept clean and warm, offered food and water by mouth, and that nothing is done to intentionally end her life.

A living will may, or may not, designate a surrogate or surrogates to make medical decisions for the patient that are not addressed in the document itself. A child or two children, for instance, may be named as surrogates for a father or mother, or a husband as surrogate for a wife. If the living will is very comprehensive and adequately expresses all the patients' wishes, a surrogate may not be needed.

Living wills must be signed in front of at least one witness, and the definition of an acceptable witness varies from state to state. Generally, a witness should be someone other than a health care provider or a family member or anyone else who may have a financial interest in the patient's estate. Some states also required that a living will be notarized.

Many living wills include a section that releases doctors from legal liability for withholding measures that may possibly prolong life. This is to prevent family members from coming back and suing a doctor for not doing everything in his power to save Mom's life.

Medical Power of Attorney

A medical power of attorney is a document that allows an individual to appoint someone else to make decisions about his medical care if he's unable to communicate. The difference between a medical power of attorney and a living will, which also may appoint someone to make decisions, is that a medical power of attorney does not focus primarily on end-of-life issues. There are various situations other than those that occur at the end of life in which your parent might need a surrogate to make decisions concerning her health care. For instance:

- Mom is injured in a car accident and the doctors say she may remain unconscious for hours, or even days.
- Dad has some eye surgery that requires general anesthesia. He'll be unconscious for several hours, and probably extremely groggy for several more.
- Mom was diagnosed with Alzheimer's disease three years ago, and is

completely incapable of making decisions concerning her medical care.

- Dad's had a stroke and is unable to speak or express himself in any way.

The person appointed in the medical power of attorney to make decisions if the patient is unable to do so might be called a health care agent, a surrogate, an attorney-in-fact, or a proxy. Many people also appoint an alternate agent or agents as backup.

Obviously, choosing a health care proxy is something your parent should think about carefully before making a decision. The proxy should be someone she trusts completely, and who understands and will honor all her wishes and decisions. Preferably, he should live fairly close in order to be able to be available when necessary, and be someone in whose judgment and wisdom your mother has confidence. The proxy also must be willing to serve. Don't assume that your older brother is willing to be Mom's proxy. Many people are reluctant to assume responsibility for making medical decisions for another person, even if those decisions are spelled out in a legal document.

Duties of a Health Care Proxy

If Mom chooses you as her health care proxy, or as a surrogate to make end-of-life decisions in the event that she's terminally ill or incapacitated, you'll need to be aware of what the job entails. Your first responsibility as proxy should be to sit down with your mother and talk about her wishes, concerns, and fears. Some of these will be expressed in her living will or medical power of attorney, but others may not be. You'll be working with health-care providers to ensure that your mother's wishes are honored, so it's extremely important that you're sure you fully understand exactly what Mom wants.

Maybe your mother has a real fear, for instance, of dying alone, or greatly desires to die at home. Maybe she's terribly afraid that she won't be able to maintain her dignity, or that she'll be a bother to her family and health care providers. Or, she may be terribly afraid that she'll spend the end of her life in terrible pain. This type of information may be included in an advance directive, but often is not. Knowing her feelings about these kinds of issues makes it easier for you to help her, and can give you peace of mind by knowing that you did everything you could to make her comfortable and put her mind at ease. It's not easy to talk about these kinds of issues, but it can be a great gift to both your mother and yourself if you do.

A friend served as her father's health care surrogate for end-of-life decisions and a year later still wonders if she made the right choices, even though she explicitly followed the instructions in his living will. Many people have a tendency to second-guess themselves after a loved one dies, even when they know they've acted according to his wishes. Learning as much as you can about your parent's attitudes and wishes before you need to make difficult choices can make the job of being a surrogate a little easier.

If Mom's health is not great and she's under the frequent or constant care of a doctor, you should make it a point, as her proxy, to get to know the doctor. Tell him what your role is, and that you'll be overseeing her care in order to be sure that her wishes are followed. If Mom is incapacitated, be sure the doctor has seen a copy of her living will and ask him if he's prepared to follow her instructions as stated. Although most doctors comply with instructions stated in legal advance directives, they are not required by law to follow those directions if they oppose them on moral or ethical grounds.

Even if your mother is completely capable of communicating with her doctor, don't assume that she's doing so. Many people, especially older ones, feel that they shouldn't question a doctor, and are afraid to ask questions or challenge the need for a particular medical treatment. And, as stated earlier, many people don't understand that they have the right to refuse any medical treatment they don't want.

Working With Health Care Providers

In order to be effective as your mother's health care proxy or surrogate, or just to be able to advocate for her as a son or daughter, you should learn as much as you can about her condition. You can learn a lot about particular diseases from good medical books or Internet sites, and that's a great way to get a background about Mom's condition. To learn about her specific condition, however, you'll need to talk to her doctors. Chances are that she'll have more doctors than just her primary physician, and it's a good idea for you to have their names, phone numbers, and areas of specialty.

Ask her various doctors about your mother's illness, their plans for treating her, and the possible or expected outcomes of the treatments. Don't be afraid to ask about alternate treatments. Find out what types of drugs will be prescribed, and make sure each doctor your mother sees knows every type of medicine she's taking. Many, many people have suffered severe adverse effects from taking medications that don't mix, and it's often because one doctor doesn't know what another has prescribed.

The American Medical Association's website, accessible at www.ama-assn.org, contains a section for patients that includes information about various diseases. Another useful site is the Centers for Disease Control and Prevention, located on the web at www.cdc.gov.

Make a list of all the questions you want to ask the doctor, and keep the list with you when you accompany Mom to her appointment, or when you're at the hospital, nursing home, or other medical facility. Make notes concerning any problems she's told you about or that you've noticed yourself. A doctor should be willing to take time to talk you to, and you should be prepared when he does. If you don't have time to talk with the doctor during or after the appointment, ask if you could call him later to follow up on some questions you have.

While you have a right to expect information from a doctor, you also have a responsibility to see that he gets all the information he needs. If your mother's not able to effectively communicate with the doctor about her condition, you may have to do it for her. Make sure he knows of any chronic health problems she may have, and bring along results of any recent tests she may have had. Have a list and the dose amounts of all medicines she takes—that includes prescription drugs, over the counter medications, and vitamins or herbal remedies. If you know of any drug allergies or other problems concerning medications, be sure you mention those to the doctor. He needs to have all the information possible about your mother in order to be able to help her effectively.

If Mom is able to communicate with the doctor herself, remind her that it's important that she shares all the applicable information and asks any questions she might have. Many older patients feel that they should not question a doctor, and they do whatever he advises without even knowing why the treatment has been prescribed.

Some other suggestions for effectively communicating with doctors are listed below.

- Don't rush or be rushed. Don't skip over parts of questions you want to ask because you feel like you're taking up too much of the doctor's time. Follow up on your questions until you fully understand what's going on. You'll be much more help to Mom if you know what's happening.

- Ask the doctor to talk so you can understand him. If the doctor is using medical terms that you don't understand, ask him to re-explain it in language you can understand. Don't feel stupid if you can't understand his medical jargon, and don't nod your head and say you understand what he's saying if you don't.
- If you make an appointment to speak to a doctor, don't be late. This is a particular gripe of physicians, who tend to be very busy.
- Expect that the doctor will treat you, and your mother, with the respect that you deserve. If he doesn't, say so.
- If a doctor doesn't seem to understand your concerns, or doesn't seem to be taking those concerns seriously, explain to him why you feel they're important.
- If you're having real trouble communicating with a doctor, see if there is a social worker or patient representative available to help you. They often are able to assist in such matters.
- If you can't get any satisfaction from your dealings with a doctor, don't be afraid to speak to someone who is his superior. That could be the chief of staff, a risk manager, or hospital administrator.

While doctors certainly are important to your mother's health care, they're not the only health-care providers with whom you'll have contact. Nurses may be more accessible, and usually have been trained to work with patients and their families. They can talk with you about treatment options, explain a diagnosis, teach you how to help Mom with tasks such as taking her blood pressure or giving herself injections.

Pharmacists can be invaluable when it comes to questions and concerns about prescription drugs. They have information about drug interactions, doses, side effects, and so forth, and usually are willing to take time to help you. If you're overwhelmed by the health care system, need help figuring out an insurance matter, or have questions about moving Mom into a rehab facility or other treatment center, a social worker probably can help you. Most hospitals have social workers, as do many nursing homes and treatment facilities. And, dieticians can provide information on nutrition and special diets to accommodate various conditions.

Ideally, Mom should have a health care team, not a group of people administering care independently without knowing what the others are doing. You can facilitate that team approach by keeping each caregiver informed.

Managing Medicine

Prescription medicines are likely to be an important part of Dad's health care, not to mention a significant impact on his pocketbook. Although prescription drugs were mentioned in Chapter Two and throughout this chapter, the topic is significant enough to be addressed in a bit more depth.

As you read in Chapter Two, the cost of prescription drugs rose 17.4 percent in 2000. That's about 15 percent more than the general cost of inflation for that year. In five years, between 1993 and 1998, the average cost of prescription drugs increased by 40 percent. Reports show that about one third of all senior citizens do not have prescription coverage, forcing many to choose between buying drugs and the other things that they need. Many of the Medicare managed care plan that used to cover the cost of some prescription drugs have reduced or eliminated those benefits. Even many seniors whose insurance does cover prescription drugs are paying more as their co-pays increase.

So, why do prescription drugs cost so much? Drug manufacturers will tell you that they're simply passing along the high costs of research and development. Critics, however, say that the manufacturers spend more each year on marketing and advertising than they do on research and development. They also say that major drug companies pay manufacturers of generic drugs millions of dollars to keep the generic drugs out of the market, and that drug companies are turning huge profits, even as they complain of high costs.

Government and consumer groups are looking into these matters and putting pressure on the drug companies to reduce their costs; senior and consumer groups are putting pressure on the politicians to have some form of prescription medicine price relief. There is bipartisan support in Congress for a change, and President Bush has made a federal prescription medicine program part of his agenda.

Saving Money on Prescriptions

While we wait for the cost of prescription drugs to level off, there are some steps your parents can take to save money on prescription medicines. They include:

- Government programs for people with low income. These vary from state to state, but there are programs that assist low-income seniors who need prescription drugs. There usually is a co-pay, but the programs cover the majority of the cost. Contact your local area agency on aging to find out what might be available in your state.

- Discount cards. The American Association of Retired Persons offers a card that gives seniors discounts on prescription drugs in more than 45,000 drug stores across the country. The card costs $15 a year, and those who use it report that they save an average of $167 a year. K-Mart offers a free card that gives seniors up to 40 percent savings in K-Mart pharmacies.
- Some online pharmacies offer price discounts on prescription drugs. Check out sites such as www.drugstore.com or www.webrx.com.
- Nearly all of the major drug companies give discounted or free medicine to needy people who apply. Requirements for participation in these programs varies from company to company. Your doctor probably has a form you can fill out to see if you qualify.
- Ask your doctor if there's a lower-priced drug that provides the same benefits as the more expensive one you're currently taking. There sometimes is a big difference in cost between brand-name drugs that are in the same categories.
- Buy the smallest amount of medicine you can when starting a new one. If it turns out you have a reaction or have to stop taking it for another reason, you won't have wasted money on a month's supply of pills that you can't use.
- See if there's a different strength tablet or capsule that costs less. It seems strange, but there's sometimes a big difference in cost. If you're taking two 50 m.g. tablets a day, for instance, you might be able to get 100 m.g. tablets for less money and simply take one a day.

Despite the ever-increasing costs of prescription drugs, it's estimated that at least two thirds of all senior citizens take at least one. Many have multiple prescriptions, and that can be the cause of serious problems.

Watching Out For Drug Trouble

Elderly people react to medicine differently than younger people do. Higher levels of active ingredients enter the bloodstreams in elderly people than in younger ones, due to the level of muscle mass and other factors. As a result, one medication may cause more of a reaction, and many older people are taking three, four, or more medications every day.

If that's the case, you should be aware of the possibility of problems. The medicines may interact with each other and cause adverse reactions, or there's the possibility that they could neutralize each other. This is why it's important that your parents, or you, if they're not able to, let their doctors know exactly what—and how much—they're taking before he prescribes another drug. Your parents should never take each other's medications or borrow drugs from a friend or relative. They should take the prescribed dosage for as long as the doctor tells them they need it. Many people try to get around the high cost of prescription medicine by taking less that what's been prescribed for them, or taking it every other day instead of every day.

A problem elderly people commonly encounter is not being able to remember if they've taken their medicine. If this is a problem for your parent, you can buy a pill dispenser and fill it with all their medications for a whole week. That way, Dad only has to take the pills that are in the dispenser for the particular day. Be careful though if you do that, because it may be that some pills are to be taken in the morning, and others at night.

The Journal of the American Medical Association has posted a list of prescription drugs that commonly cause problems in elderly people. The side effects of each drug varies, but if your parent is taken any of the drugs listed below, you should keep a watch out for possible adverse reactions. Drugs included in the journal are listed below.

Sedatives or sleeping agents: Diazepam, Chlordiazepoxide, Flurazepam, Meprobamate, Pentobarbital, Secobarbital
Antidepressant: Amitriptyline
Nonsteroidal anti-inflammatory drugs: Indomethacin, Phenylbutazone
Oral diabetes drug: Chlorpropamide
Analgesics: Propoxyplene, Pentazocine
Dementia treatments: Isoxsuprine, Cyclandelate
Platelet inhibitor: Dipyridamole
Muscle relaxants: Cyclobenzaprine, Methocarbamol, Carisoprodol, Orphenadrine

To find out more about these and other prescription drugs, one of the books you can check out is called *1,001 Prescription Drugs: Side Effects, Dangerous Combinations, and Natural Healing Alternatives for Seniors*. It's by the editors at FC&A Medical Publishing and available in bookstores or from online booksellers. Or, you can find information, including possible side effects, for hundreds of prescription medicines on line at www.focusonmedications.com.

For many seniors, prescription medicines are a part of life. Indeed, these drugs improve the quality of life for millions of people every day. If your parents are constantly worried about how much their drugs cost or how they're going to pay for them, however, the prescriptions may seem to be as much of a problem as a cure.

Reassure your parents that you'll help them to try to save money on their prescriptions, and keep an eye on legislative news so you'll be aware of any new measures to assist senior citizens. Let them talk about their concerns while encouraging them to use the medicines as prescribed.

Helping With Mom and Dad's Health Care from Long Distance

If you live in Denver and your parents are in Virginia, chances are you're not as involved with their health care as you would be if you lived just around the corner. There are steps you can take, however, to stay informed about their care and to assist when possible.

Make sure you have the names and phone numbers of all Mom and Dad's doctors so you can contact them if necessary. If your mother calls you one night and tells you Dad's had a stroke and is in the hospital, you'll no doubt want to phone his doctor to get a report on his condition. Also keep a list of numbers for hospitals and other applicable facilities in their area.

If Dad is having persistent or serious health problems, you might want to schedule a visit around his next doctor's appointment. This would give you a chance to ask questions and bring up issues that may not occur to Dad. This would be especially helpful if you know he has some medical tests coming up, or is scheduled for some sort of procedure.

Another area in which you can be very useful from long distance is helping your parents with their medical bills and statements. Taking charge of this chore would be a great help to a sibling who lives close by and is taking the bulk of responsibility for caring for Mom and Dad. Or, if your parents are taking care of their medical bills on their own, chances are they'd welcome the help.

If you're handling your parents' medical paperwork from out of town, send them large envelopes that are already addressed and include postage. They can put all their bills and statements in the envelope and send it right back to you.

If you're in a financial position to do so, you could consider hiring a geriatric care manager to help your parents when you're unable to, and to serve as a liaison between your parents and you. Although different geriatric care managers offer different services, many will visit your parents at regular intervals and report back to you concerning their medical situations, condition of their home, whether or not they seemed to be confused, and so forth. As you can imagine, this can provide significant peace of mind to children who live far away from aging parents.

As you learned in Chapter Two, geriatric care managers also can arrange for home care workers, help your parents to get to and from appointments, oversee moving your parents into assisted care or another type of facility if it becomes necessary, and sort through medical, financial, and household papers. These types of services, unfortunately, are not covered by insurance at this point, so you'd have to pay for them yourself.

Chapter Five

Understanding Your Parents' Health Care Coverage

Spend an hour or so with a group of senior citizens and the conversation almost inevitably will turn to health and health care. These are incredibly important topics to most older people. Many seniors deal with health and health-related issues nearly every day—with good reason. If they're not battling health and health-related problems themselves, they no doubt know plenty of folks who are. Let's look at a few examples of the kinds of issues older people face regularly.

Your mom's bridge partner has a stroke. She spends a week and a half in the hospital and then goes to a rehabilitation center for another two weeks. Her insurance won't cover any more time in the rehab center, but her doctor tells her she's not ready to return to her apartment, where she lives alone. She could go to her son's house for a few weeks, but he and his wife both work and she'd be alone there for most of the time, anyway. Besides, she finds it a bit difficult to be around her son for more than a couple of hours at a time. What is she supposed to do?

An elderly woman who lives in your neighborhood suffers from terrible arthritis pain, but hasn't been able to find a medicine that significantly relieves it. She has trouble sleeping at night because of the pain, and as a result spends much of the day dozing in a chair. She rarely goes out anymore because her left leg has a tendency to give out on her and she's afraid of falling. Finally, her doctor gives her a prescription for a new arthritis medicine, which he believes will make her feel much better. The problem is, the pills will cost $60 a week, and there's no way she can afford to buy it. What's the answer?

Your dad's buddy has a heart attack while he's playing tennis, and ends up with a triple bypass operation. He recovers faster and more easily than expected, and can't wait to get out of the hospital and back into his own house. The problem is, the doctor says he needs therapy, and his insurance won't cover in-home treatment. He ends up having to go to a nursing home that has an approved therapy treatment center, and he hates every minute that he's there. How could this have been handled differently?

These and thousands more situations like them occur every day, leaving elderly people and their families upset, angry, and frustrated. Many older people (younger ones too, for that matter) don't understand the complexities of their insurance plans. Often, older people tend to be less willing than younger ones to question their doctors or their insurance carriers about health and health care issues. Some are afraid they'll lose the coverage they have if they make waves.

Health care is a hot topic in America, there's no question about it. Right now, partisan politics are delaying a patients' bill of rights, but some form of bill should be passed in the near future. If and when it passes, the bill is meant to achieve these goals:

- Allow doctors—not insurance companies—to make medical decisions affecting patients.
- Allow patients to sue their health plan providers if the providers make decisions that end up causing harm to the patient.
- Give patients more choices in choosing doctors and specialists.
- Give patients the right of appeal if care is denied or delayed.

This proposed legislation reflects the increasing concerns of many, many Americans who are concerned about their health care coverage—or lack of coverage. At the end of 1998, there were 43 million people in this country with no health insurance, according to a CNN report. Millions more who do have coverage worry about uncovered expenses, the increasing costs of prescription medicine, and whether they may be dropped by their insurers.

Fortunately, most people over 65 are covered by Medicare, a health insurance program administered by the Centers for Medicare and Medicaid Service. Low-income seniors may be covered by Medicaid, which is a state-administered, but funded by state and federal governments, program.

In this chapter, you'll learn about these programs, and other benefits for which your parents may be eligible. We'll also take a look at the controversial topic of long-term health care insurance, and who may benefit from that. Let's start by taking a good look at Medicare, and how it operates.

Understanding Medicare

Medicare is the country's largest health insurance program, covering 39 million Americans. President Bush has announced that he plans to overhaul the program during his term as president, although the specifics of his plan are not yet known. He did say that he wants Medicare to include prescription drug benefits, which at this time it does not.

Currently, three groups of people are eligible for Medicare. They are:

1. Those who are 65 years or older
2. Some people who are under 65 and disabled
3. People with end-stage renal disease, which means there is permanent kidney failure, requiring either dialysis or a kidney transplant

In addition, in 2001, Congress passed a new law that allows people under age 65 who have Amytrophic Lateral Sclerosis (also known as Lou Gehrig's disease) to get Medicare benefits.

Let's take a look first at how someone goes about getting signed up for Medicare benefits. Then, we'll see how Medicare works. Many people don't realize that there are two parts to the program, and that the parts cover different types of services.

Getting Signed Up

Fortunately for most people, sign-up for the Medicare program is automatic. If your dad is already getting Social Security benefits and he's about to turn 65, he doesn't need to do a thing. He'll be automatically enrolled in Medicare the month that he turns 65. If his birthday is May 19, for instance, his benefits will kick in May 1. If his birthday is on the first day of a month, his benefits begin the first day of the preceding month.

If he's turning 65 but isn't getting Social Security, he can apply for both Social Security and Medicare at the same time. Ideally, he should do this three months before he turns 65. He can apply up until four months after his birthday, but some Medicare coverage might be delayed. To apply, Dad can stop by or call his local Social Security office, or he can call Social Security at 1-800-772-1213. He may even be able to apply on line, if he uses a computer and has access to the Internet. Social Security is located on line at www.ssa.gov.

If Dad is about to turn 65, is not getting Social Security, and wants to apply only for Medicare, he can do that, too. Just as if he was applying for both benefits, he should contact his local Social Security office or call the 800 number listed above, and he should do so three months before his 65th birthday.

The Two Parts of Medicare

Medicare comes in two flavors: Part A and Part B. Basically, Part A is the hospital insurance part of Medicare, while Part B is commonly called the medical insurance part. A big difference between the two parts is that B (medical insurance) is optional, while A (hospital insurance) is not.

Everyone is automatically enrolled in Part B when they become eligible for Part A. If Mom and Dad are still covered by Dad's company insurance, for instance, they might not need the benefits of Medicare's Part B. Everyone, however, should be signed up for Part A, and make sure your parents don't wait until one of them is in the hospital to try to get enrolled. The Medicare people really don't like that, and getting signed up when you're already hospitalized is a real hassle that involves a ton of paperwork and some delays that can cause big problems at an already stressful time.

Medicare certainly is a blessing to millions of senior citizens. There are some things, however, that aren't covered, at least not as this time. They include: nearly all prescription drugs; most dental care and dentures; routine eye exams, physical exams, and foot care; orthopedic shoes; hearing aids; help with everyday tasks such as dressing or bathing; and cosmetic surgery.

Part A is extremely important for seniors, due to the terribly high cost of staying in the hospital. In 1998, the average hospital bill ranged from $9,243 in Oregon (that was the lowest average cost) to $18,781 in Nevada (the highest average cost). Those being average costs, you can imagine what a hospital stay of several months in 2002 would cost. Few people have hundreds of thousands of dollars to spend on a lengthy hospital stay, so you can see how important this part of Medicare is. Mom will have to pay some deductibles, just like with almost any insurance plan, and she'll have to pay for non-medical aspects of a hospital stay, such as the cost for a television and phone in her room.

A list of items and services covered by Part A of Medicare are listed below:
- Hospital Stays: includes a semi-private room, meals, general nursing and other hospital services, and supplies. Inpatient health care coverage in a psychiatric facility is limited to 190 days in a lifetime.
- Skilled Nursing Facility: includes a semi-private room, meals, skilled nursing and rehabilitative services, and other services and supplies. You must have a three-day hospital stay before being approved for a skilled nursing facility.

- Home Health Care: part-time skilled nursing care; physical, occupational, or speech-language therapy; home health aide services; medical equipment such as wheelchairs, walkers, oxygen, or hospital beds; and other services.
- Hospice Care: under certain conditions, this includes medical or support services from a Medicare-approved hospice; drugs for symptom control and pain relief; short-term respite care, care in a hospice facility, hospital, or nursing home when necessary; home hospice care; and other services.
- Blood: that given to the patient during a covered hospital or skilled nursing facility stay.

This part of Medicare is free, but patients covered by Part A may be responsible for some of the costs of the covered services. For instance, at 2001 rates, Dad would have to pay a deductible of $812 for a hospital stay of one to 60 days, then $203 per day for days 61 through 90 of a hospital stay, and $406 a day after 60 days. If he went to a skilled nursing facility and his stay there qualified for Medicare coverage, he'd pay nothing for the first 20 days, but would have to pay up to $101.50 a day for days 21 through 100.

If Mom is getting at-home health care and needs to have a hospital bed and oxygen, she'll be charged for 20 percent of the cost of the equipment, although she'll pay nothing for the services. If she required inpatient psychiatric hospital care, she'd have to pay a $800 hospital deductible per benefit period (at 2002 rates).

Part B of the Medicare program covers doctors' services (but not routine physicals), and services such as blood tests, treatment of an injury or illness, outpatient hospital services, and supplies such as wheelchairs, hospital beds, and oxygen. Some home health care services also are covered by this plan. A list of services covered by Part B is below:
- Medical and Other Services: doctors' services (except routine physicals), outpatient medical and surgical services and supplies, diagnostic tests, ambulatory surgery center facility fees (for approved procedures), medical equipment such as wheelchairs, hospital beds, oxygen, and walkers. Also covers outpatient physical and occupational therapy, and outpatient mental health services.
- Clinical Laboratory Services: blood tests, urinalysis, and so forth.
- Home Health Care: Part-time skilled care, home health aide services,

medical equipment that's supplied by a home health agency, and other supplies and services.

- Outpatient Hospital Services: Services required for the diagnosis or treatment of an illness or injury.
- Blood: Pints of blood as needed as an outpatient, or during services performed that are covered by Part B
- Hospice Care: Medical and support services from a Medicare-approved hospice for people with terminal illnesses and drugs for pain relief or symptom control.

Part B also covers some preventive services (although the patient may have to pay a portion of the cost), including: bone mass measurement, colorectal cancer screening, diabetes monitoring, mammogram screening, pap smear and pelvic exam, prostate cancer screening, and vaccinations, including flu and pneumonia shots.

For most people, Part B is a little bit harder to deal with, financially. Mom will need to pay a deductible of $100 each year, and a monthly premium of $54 (2002 rates), that will be automatically taken out of her Social Security check. On top of that, she may need to chip in another 20 to 50 percent of the bill, depending on what services have been performed. For instance, she'll pay 20 percent of her physical therapy costs if she needs rehabilitation following a stroke, and will have to come up with 50 percent if she needs outpatient mental health services. As you can imagine, those combined costs can add up quickly. To insure them against the costs those extra costs, most people buy Medigap insurance.

Medigap Insurance

Medigap, as it's become known, is private insurance that picks up some of the services and equipment that Medicare doesn't cover. It's a supplemental insurance that pays the cost of co-payments, premiums, deductibles, and the doctor's bills that are more than what Medicare approves.

As a note, Medicare tries to keep its costs reasonable by setting amounts that it will pay for each service. For instance, Medicare might decide that it will pay $150 for a specific test. Most doctors (about 70 percent) participate in the Medicare program, which means that they would accept $150 for the test.

Doctors who participate in the program are called "participating physicians," and are said to "accept assignment" when they take the $150 that Medicare offers. If a doctor doesn't accept assignment because he wants to charge more for that test, Mom or Dad will be responsible for making up the difference. If the doctor charges $165 instead of $150, Mom will have to pay the 20 percent co-pay, plus the extra $15. Fortunately for senior citizens, doctors are permitted to charge only 15 percent more than what Medicare assigns, and some states prohibit them from charging any more. Even 15 percent above an already-high cost for a specialized test or treatment, however, can be significant.

It certainly is within your rights, and the rights of your parents, to ask whether a certain doctor is a participating physician in the Medicare program. Not all Medigap plans cover these extra fees, and you don't want Mom and Dad to end up with a lot of extra medical bills.

Some, but not all, Medigap programs cover excess doctors fees. And, Medigap rarely covers anything that Medicare doesn't address, such as dental care (other than that done during a hospital stay) or routine eye exams. It might pick up the co-pay and some of the deductibles, but it won't pay for a service that Medicare doesn't cover.

To make the Medigap terrain easier to navigate, states limit Medigap to 10 plans from which to choose. They're labeled Plan A through Plan J, with Plan J being the most comprehensive—and the most expensive.

This ten-plan option makes life a lot easier for most people. Trying to figure out how much coverage you need, or can afford, can be difficult. With the ten-plan program, Mom can look at the benefits and cost of each plan and choose the one that best fits her needs. This can help her avoid paying unnecessarily for coverage she won't use. Most states offer a few of the standardized plans as Medicare Select. That's a type of Medigap plan that costs less because it requires patients to use specific hospitals and doctors (except if it's an emergency) in order to get their full benefits.

You can help your parents learn more about these Medigap plans by going to www.medicare.gov/MGCompare. This is Medicare's website, which offers lists of companies in each state that offer the various Medigap programs. Or, Mom and Dad can get a free copy of the Guide to Health Insurance for People With Medicare by calling 1-800-633-4227.

Let's take a look at what is covered by the ten standard Medigap plans. Prices for the plan will vary depending on the company from which your parents buy the plan, the state in which they live, and so forth.

- **Plan A:** basic benefits.
- **Plan B:** basic benefits, inpatient hospital deductible (Part A).
- **Plan C:** basic benefits, inpatient hospital deductible (Part A), skilled-nursing facility co-pay (Part A), standard deduction (Part B), foreign travel emergency.
- **Plan D:** basic benefits, inpatient hospital deductible (Part A), skilled-nursing facility co-pay (Part A), foreign travel emergency, personal care at home.
- **Plan E:** basic benefits, inpatient hospital deductible (Part A), skilled-nursing facility co-pay (Part A), foreign travel emergency, preventive care.
- **Plan F:** basic benefits, inpatient hospital deductible (Part A), skilled-nursing facility co-pay (Part A), standard deduction (Part B), foreign travel emergency, 100% of excess charges (Part B).
- **Plan G:** basic benefits, inpatient hospital deductible (Part A), skilled-nursing facility co-pay (Part A), foreign travel emergency, personal care at home, 80% of excess charges (Part B).
- **Plan H:** basic benefits, inpatient hospital deductible (Part A), skilled-nursing facility co-pay (Part A), foreign travel emergency, prescription drugs.
- **Plan I:** basic benefits, inpatient hospital deductible (Part A), skilled-nursing facility co-pay (Part A), foreign travel emergency, personal care at home, 100% of excess charges (Part B), prescription drugs.
- **Plan J:** basic benefits, inpatient hospital deductible (Part A), skilled-nursing facility co-pay (Part A), standard deduction (Part B), foreign travel emergency, personal care at home, 100% of excess charges (Part B), preventive care, prescription drugs.

It should be noted that plans F and J have a high-deductible option that brings their costs down. While this information gives a general overview of the Medigap plans, your parents should get a copy of Medicare's guide for more complete information. There are a lot of companies out there trying to sell Medigap insurance, and not all of them have only your parents' best interests in mind. The more information Mom and Dad have, the more qualified they'll be to make decisions.

If they need help choosing a Medigap policy, or with any Medicare-related issue, they can find it at SHIP (Seniors Health Insurance Program). Counselors there offer free advice with Medicare and Medigap issues. Mom and Dad can contact their local SHIP program through the area agency on aging.

Tips to Remember When Buying Medigap

Here are some tips that your parents should keep in mind when shopping for Medigap insurance. They're provided by Consumer Insurance Advocate, Inc., a California-based agency.

- Shop Carefully Before Buying. As you can see from the list above, policies vary greatly, both in cost and coverage. Your parents should contact different insurance companies and compare the premiums before they buy. And, they should remember to consider what kind of service various companies offer, too.
- Don't Buy More Policies Than Are Necessary. Duplicate coverage can be expensive and is unnecessary. A single comprehensive policy is better than several policies that overlap or duplicate coverage. Federal law prohibits an insurer from selling someone a second Medigap policy unless the person states in writing that he intends to cancel the policy he already has. Anyone who sells you a policy in violation of federal law.
- Watch Out For Pre-existing Condition Exclusions. When buying Medigap insurance, it's important that your parents do so within the first six months after they hit 65 years old and enroll in Part B of Medicare. If they catch this open enrollment period, the insurance company from which they're buying can't deny coverage or change the price of a policy because of past or current health problems. If they don't enroll during that time, they may have to pay more for coverage, or be denied coverage.
- Use Care When Replacing an Existing Policy. Don't jump around from policy to policy. Your parents should change only if they need to change in order to get different benefits, better service, or a better price. But, don't keep inadequate policies just because you've had them for a long time. If they decide to replace their Medigap policy, they must be given credit for the time spent under the old policy in determining whether, and to what extent, any pre-existing conditions restrictions apply under the new policy. They also will have to sign a statement that they intend to terminate the policy they're replacing. However, they have 30 days to cancel, so they shouldn't cancel the first policy until they're sure they want to keep the new one. Make sure that the insurance plan can be put in place and delivered within 30 days.

- Don't be pressured. It's against the law for a company or agent to use high-pressure tactics to force or frighten anyone into buying a Medigap policy or to make fraudulent or misleading comparisons to make someone switch from one company or policy to another. Your parents should take time to examine available policies, then choose the one they want.
- Know that Medigap Policies Are Not Government Policies. State insurance departments approve policies that private insurance companies sell, but state or federal governments don't sell or administer Medigap plans. Some people wrongly assume that Medigap is a government program because Medicare is.
- Make Sure the Insurance Company is Qualified in Your State. A company must meet certain qualifications in order to be certified within a particular state. Have your parents check with their state insurance department to confirm that a company with which they're considering dealing is licensed. Agents also must be licensed by the state.
- Complete the Application Carefully. It's very important that the medical history part of an insurance application is carefully completed. If any information is left out, coverage could be refused for a period of time for any medical condition that wasn't mentioned. The company also could deny a claim for treatment of an undisclosed condition and/or cancel your policy.
- Understand the Policy. Buyers must be given a clearly worded summary of the policy. Make sure Mom and Dad read it carefully and understand it.
- Don't Pay Cash. Your parents should pay for the policy with a check, money order or bank draft made payable to the insurance company—not to the agent or anyone else. Make sure they get a receipt that includes the insurance company's name, address, and telephone number. Deal with an agent who provides service and will help with any forms that need to be completed, answer questions, and generally help your parents deal with the paperwork.

Other Options for Medicare

While most people choose to enroll in the original Medicare program, your parents have some Medicare options. They can join a managed care program instead of the original Medicare program if they're so inclined, or choose to participate in a private fee-for-service plan.

The managed care Medicare is an HMO, under which Mom and Dad would have to use a set network of doctors, hospitals, rehabs, nursing homes, and clinics. They would only be able to choose doctors who participate in the HMO, and they must get pre-approval for specialists and other services. Medicare pays the HMO a certain amount of money every year to cover Mom and Dad. What the HMO doesn't spend, it gets to keep.

Many people don't like having their choices limited, but there are some advantages to the managed care plan. First of all, it eliminates the need for Medigap insurance. Mom and Dad would pay a monthly fee to the managed care company, but it's usually less than a Medigap policy. Another advantage is that managed care Medicare usually covers items and services such as dental care, prescription drugs, glasses, and hearing aids.

By law, these HMOs must offer everything that the original Medicare program does, and, the HMO takes care of the paperwork.

Another fairly new alternative is the private fee-for-service plan. This is when Medicare pays a private insurance company to take care of Mom and Dad, and the insurance company decides how much they'll have to pay for the services they receive.

These Medicare options are further explained on Medicare's website (www.medicare.gov). You can see a comparison of managed care programs and check out Your Guide to Private Fee-For-Service Plans.

Appealing a Medicare Decision

We've all heard horror stories about people who have been denied health services, or were sent home from the hospital still sick to a family that was not equipped to care for them.

A friend's father had a severe stroke. Emergency response personnel (911) sent out an ambulance, and then dispatched a second one containing life support equipment when they fully learned the seriousness of the man's condition. Medicare refused to pay for the ambulance that contained the life support equipment, saying that it wasn't necessary. The family appealed the decision and won.

If you feel that Medicare has not treated your parent fairly, you can help Mom or Dad to appeal the decision. The directions for how to do so are on the back of the form that explains their benefits. If you feel that Mom is being sent home from the hospital too early, contact your state's Peer Review Organization. This is a physician watchdog group that the federal government contracts to monitor Medicare patients' hospital care. The hospital must give you the phone number for the Peer Review Organization if you request it. And, it must keep Mom there while her case is being reviewed.

Taking on a bureaucracy like Medicare can certainly seem daunting, but, it's well worth the trouble. The Health Care Financing Administration, the group that manages the Medicare Program, estimates that 70 percent of cases appealed result in some compensation for the patient. If you appeal a Medicare decision, don't pay any bills to Medicare until the case has been resolved.

Understanding Medicaid

While the two sometimes are confused, Medicare and Medicaid are two very different programs.

Medicaid is a government health program that was originally designed for helping people who live at, or below the legal poverty level. Medicaid is administered by the states, so the rules concerning the program vary from state to state. Each state establishes its own eligibility standards; determines the type, amount, duration, and scope of services; sets the payment rate for services; and administers its own program.

If your parents have limited assets, it's probably a good idea to learn more about Medicaid. Even if they are fairly comfortable financially, but you think one or both of them might require long-term care (such as a nursing home), you should start thinking ahead. Many people think they'll never need Medicaid, only to learn that long-term care can drain a savings account very quickly.
- All Medicaid patients are entitled to the following benefits:
- Inpatient and outpatient hospital services
- Doctor services
- Periodic diagnostic tests and screenings
- Laboratory and x-ray services
- Rural health clinic services
- Nursing home care
- In-home health care (for those who qualify)
- Medical transportation

Medicaid programs in some states also cover dental and eye care, prescription drugs, glasses, hospice care, and other goods and services. A problem associated with Medicaid is that some doctors and nursing homes don't accept Medicaid patients because the reimbursements they receive from Medicaid are low. Medicaid patients are sometimes forced to scramble around to find treatment, and sometimes have to settle for less-than-great care.

Knowing if Your Parents are Eligible

There are lawyers who specialize in Medicaid planning, and, if you think your parents may need Medicaid in the future, it's a good idea to meet with such a lawyer as early as possible. There are some basic, federal guidelines concerning Medicaid, but other rules vary widely from state to state. In some states, for instance, a spouse can refuse to pay nursing home costs for his or her partner, and gets to keep all of his or her income. In other states, a spouse gets to keep whatever assets are necessary to pay his or her regular bills—regardless of what they may be for. If your parents can't afford to pay for a lawyer, contact your state's legal services office to learn about legal aid for the elderly.

Many people think they won't be eligible for Medicaid until they've spent every cent they have and sold their home and everything in it. That's not so. Many people may be eligible long before they think they would be. Dad's house and personal belongings, car, furniture, and life insurance policies with a cash value under a certain amount may not be considered as assets when they apply for Medicaid. They must have a limited income (again, the rules vary from state to state), and your state will consider factors such as disability and medical needs when deciding whether your parent is eligible for Medicaid.

If Mom needs to go to a nursing home and Dad is staying in their house, he's probably entitled to keep the house, his car and personal belongings, in addition to half of their combined assets (up to a certain amount). He gets to keep any income he has, and usually part of Mom's income, too. Some states will allow Dad to keep all his savings if it's necessary to provide enough income for him to pay his bills. For instance, let's say that he has $100,000 in an investment that pays him 10 percent a year. If he needs the $10,000 he's earning on that investment to pay his regular bills, he may (according to state rules) be permitted to keep the $100,000 so that he has a continuing source of income.

There are ways in which your parents may be able to protect their assets and still qualify for Medicaid. As discussed in Chapter 3, they may be able to put money in an irrevocable trust or give some of it to children in order to reduce their assets. But, remember that if Mom applies for Medicaid in order to pay for nursing home care, officials will look carefully at her financial records for the past three years, and probably longer if she's established a trust. This is called the look-back period, and officials don't take kindly to someone who applies for Medicaid after doling out large chunks of cash to family members during the past years. If she's regularly been handing out large chunks of money, she probably will be denied coverage, at least for a while.

Some people feel it's wrong to protect their assets and then use public money for their health care. Others feel that they should be entitled to keep or pass along what they've worked hard for during their lives. This is a personal decision that you and your parents will need to discuss if it becomes necessary.

Some people transfer property to a child or some other person in order to protect it. States will claim anything left in a person's estate after the person dies in order to get back what it's spent on nursing care. If the house is in your name instead of Mom's, then it can't be considered her property. These issues are complicated, which is why it's a good idea to consult with a lawyer who specializes in Medicaid planning.

Other Programs for Low-Income Seniors

If your parents don't qualify for Medicaid, but have trouble paying their Medicare premiums and deductibles, they may qualify for aid to help them pay their medical expenses.

Medicare has a prescription drug assistance program that provides discounts or free medicines to people who have trouble paying for their drugs. There also is a program called the Qualified Medicare Beneficiary (QMB) that assists people who live at, or below the poverty level. If your parents are just a bit above the poverty level (within 10 percent) they may qualify for the Specified Low-Income Medicare Beneficiary (SLMB) program. Your local area agency on aging will be able to help your parents to apply for these programs. Or, call the Medicare Hotline at 1-800-638-6833 for more information.

Health Care Benefits for Veterans

If Dad, or Mom for that matter, is a veteran, he may qualify for a variety of health care benefits, but he'll have to sign up for them. The Veterans Administration (VA) has a uniform benefits package that includes diagnostic and treatment services, rehabilitation services, mental health care and substance abuse treatment, respite and hospice care, prescriptions, emergency care in VA facilities, hospital and outpatient services, prosthetics and orthotics. Dad also may be eligible for long-term care and treatment, including nursing home care, home-based primary care, and adult day care.

To sign up for these benefits, Dad needs to get a VA Form 10-10EZ. He does this by stopping by, calling, or writing to any VA location. Or, he can download a copy of the form on line at the VA's website, www.va.gov. The form has been simplified, so Dad shouldn't have any trouble completing it. Once he has, he can drop it off or mail it to any VA health care facility. In the application, Dad has to choose the VA health care location that he most prefers to use. This can be any VA medical center or a community-based outpatient clinic where he will receive his primary care. If for some reason the preferred facility can't give Dad the care he needs, the VA will make arrangements for another VA health care facility, or a private facility if necessary, to take over care.

Having Dad fill out the 10-10EZ doesn't automatically mean that he'll get free health care, although some veterans do. Veterans with moderate incomes or above who are accepted into the VA health care system need to help pay for their care.

Basically, everyone who applies for veteran's health benefits are divided into two categories: mandatory and discretionary. Mandatory beneficiaries are those who have service-connected disabilities, were prisoners of war, World War I veterans, or have income below a certain level. If Dad falls into any of those groups, the VA must provide his hospital and outpatient care at no cost. If he's in the discretionary group, however, chances are that he'll have a co-payment for most services.

The VA further divides applicants into seven priority groups for determining eligibility for health care benefits. Someone who was injured while serving and is 50 percent or more disabled by the injury has the highest priority. Income also is considered when determining priority groups.

Veterans also may qualify for VA burial and memorial benefits, which may include burial at a military cemetery, money for burial expenses, military funeral honors, presidential memorials, and burial flags. Your funeral director should be aware of these benefits and may be able to make contacts for you. There also are VA life insurance policies available to eligible veterans.

For more information on veteran's benefits, see the VA's web site at www.va.gov. Or, you can visit your local VA benefits office. The phone number is listed in the blue pages of your phone book.

Considering Long-Term Care Insurance

Long-term care insurance is relatively new, and there's great debate about whether it's a good idea or not for most people. Critics say it's too expensive, and many people who buy it will never benefit from their policies. Advocates say that everyone should have long-term care insurance in order to protect their assets, remove the burden of having to pay for care from the family, and ensure peace of mind.

Most people tend to buy long-term health care insurance in case they have to go into a nursing home. The insurance industry will tell you that one out of every two Americans will eventually live in a nursing home. That's a misleading statistic, however, because it includes those who may spend only a week in a nursing home in order to get rehabilitation services when recovering from a fall. Many people pass through nursing homes during their lifetimes, but it's estimated that only four percent of the elderly population actually live in them.

If Mom or Dad does have to go to a nursing home to live, however, it can be financially devastating. Nursing home care can cost $4,000 a month or more, money that most people don't have available for very long.

An advantage of some types of long-term health care insurance is that it covers not only care in a nursing home, but other types of long-term care, as well. Comprehensive long-term care insurance benefits should kick in if your parents need help in their own home with daily activities such as bathing or dressing. It also should provide assisted living services in a residential setting other than their own home, and pay for community programs such as adult day care. So, even though long-term care insurance is sometimes referred to as nursing home insurance, a comprehensive policy should cover much more than nursing home care.

Experts advise that the decision of whether or not to buy long-term care insurance be part of your parents' overall financial planning. Some suggestions to consider if they're thinking about buying the insurance include the following from the American Association of Retired Persons (AARP).

- Make sure you have a good reason to buy. Your goals should be to protect your assets, minimize dependence on other family members, and control where and how you receive long-term care services.
- Long-term care insurance can be expensive, particularly for older people. Learn as much as you can about long-term care insurance and various policies, and consider your individual circumstances.

- Be wary of buying if paying for the premiums means lowering your standard of living or giving up other things you need.
- Keep in mind that you will probably be paying premiums for a number of years. Will you still be able to afford the policy if your circumstances change or if premiums increase?
- If you would quickly qualify for Medicaid if you needed long-term care, a long-term policy would not make sense for you. That is, you would spend your savings in a short time (within six months to a year) if you were paying out of pocket.
- If Mom or Dad has a family history of chronic illness, such as diabetes, cardiovascular disease, or Alzheimer's, it makes more sense to consider long-term care insurance than if everybody in the family lived to be 90 in excellent health.

Knowing Where and What to Look For in Long-term Care Policies

Long-term care policies vary greatly. Some do cover only nursing home expenses, while others only cover home care. The daily benefit limit of policies can range from $50 a day to $500 a day or more. There are different deductibles and benefit periods. Some policies offer inflation protection. Others have non-forfeiture benefits, which means that even if you stop paying your premiums you'll receive some benefit from the policy.

There are many sources for information about long-term care. Insurance companies are one source, but you need to remember that they're out to sell a product. Sources such as the AARP or the Administration on Aging provide objective information.

If your folks do decide they want to buy long-term care insurance, the AARP recommends that they look for the following features in the policy they choose. Make sure that the policy:

- Does not require prior hospitalization to receive benefits.
- Is guaranteed renewable as long as you pay the premiums. This does not mean that premiums cannot be raised.
- Offers a premium waiver while you are receiving benefits.
- Has one deductible for the life of the policy.
- Covers pre-existing conditions, without a waiting period, if these are disclosed when you apply.

- Offers five percent compound inflation protection.
- Allows policy holders to upgrade or downgrade their coverage if they can not afford premiums.

Many big life and health insurance companies, including General Electric Capital, IDS Life, State Farm, and John Hancock, sell long-term care insurance. If your parents are looking to buy, make sure they contact a reputable company with a good rating. You can find out how an insurance company performs from A.M. Best, Standard & Poor's, Weis Research, or Moody's rating services. Directories published by these services are available in most libraries, or you can access ratings from their web sites.

Some financial planners and banks also sell long-term care insurance. Some employers offer it as part of a benefits package, and some continuing care retirement communities also offer it.

Long-term care insurance is expensive, there's no question about it. And, the older your parents are, the more they'll have to pay for it. The United Seniors Health Cooperative in Washington, D.C. estimates that a 55-year-old will pay between $300 and $1,500 a year, depending on coverage. A 75-year-old just buying long-term care insurance can expect to pay between $1,000 and $6,000 a year.

Experts advise that seniors should not spend more than five percent of their income on long-term care insurance, and most advisors recommend that they buy it when they're in their mid 60s, before any illness or disability occurs.

Long-term care insurance is something of a gamble. Dad could end up paying for it for 30 years and never use it. Or, it could turn out to be a great investment. It's a good idea for him to discuss this type of insurance with a financial advisor before deciding whether or not to buy.

You should know that there are some other types of insurance plans that can help with nursing home expenses. A living needs rider added to a life insurance policy allows the policy holder to use a percentage of his death benefit while he's still living. Be sure to find out what insurance Dad has, and if there are any provisions for this type of benefit.

Chapter Six

Dealing With Where Your Parents Will Live

It may be that dealing with your aging parents' living situation won't be a big deal. They might be able to get along just fine in their own home, hiring people to do the work they can't, while keeping up with the rest themselves. Many people do very well in their own homes well into their 80s and 90s, although they may require more help maintaining the property. It's estimated that about one and one-half million people over the age of 85 live on their own, and that number will double in the next 20 years. And, researchers say that by 2020, there will be 15.2 million people who are 65 or older living by themselves.

My parents lived in our family home until my father's death in 1998 at age 77. They maintained the five-bedroom house and 6 acres of land almost entirely by themselves. Dad mowed most of the property with his old tractor, cut down trees and split the wood to use in the fireplace, removed the snow and ice from the long driveway, and patched the roof, while Mom did all of the inside work and helped outside when she could. They loved their spot in the woods and probably wouldn't have been as happy living anywhere else.

On the other hand, we've probably all known somebody who stayed in her house long after she was capable of any level of maintenance. A 90-year-old woman in my neighborhood should not be living alone in her home. Nearly blind, she basically lives in two rooms, which are filled with clutter and debris. The house is very dirty because she's not able to see well enough to do any cleaning, and she refuses to have anyone come in to help her. She has no family that I know of, gets very little company, and depends on another neighbor to do her shopping for her. She can't see well enough to do much cooking, so she eats mostly cold foods from cans, in addition to the lunch she gets each day from Meals on Wheels.

And yet, she clings to her home. It's the place she knows, even if it's filthy, dark, and smells terrible. The neighbors worry about her and check on her, but she's basically all by herself. The thought of moving is so overwhelming to her that she refuses to even contemplate it. Unless she becomes very sick or has an accident, she probably will stay in those two rooms of her house until she dies.

For most people, our homes are more than just the buildings in which we live. They're the places where we've raised—or are raising—our children. They're where we invite our friends, celebrate holidays, take off our shoes and just relax. They're safe places—places where we can laugh, or cry, or express our frustrations with the world. In short, most people are connected emotionally to their homes.

That's one reason—a big reason—why helping parents with housing issues can be so difficult. Deciding where and how they should live is a lot different than deciding whether or not they should buy a new car. Housing issues tend to be emotional and life altering.

Fortunately, there are more living options available today than there used to be. As the population ages, more and more assisted living facilities, retirement communities, and apartments for elderly people are springing up. Older people are no longer forced to stay where they are even if they can't take care of themselves, move in with a relative, or go to an "old-folk's home."

In this chapter we'll look at the options, and some of the advantages and disadvantages of each. We'll consider financial issues concerning housing, as well as safety factors and the emotional aspects connected with moving.

Figuring Out Where Your Parents Should Live

The best time to help your parents decide about housing issues is before housing becomes an issue. If you've already talked with them about what they plan to do if the time comes that they can't remain in their home, give yourself a big pat on the back. You're ahead of the game, just by having prompted Mom and Dad to start thinking about their options.

Many people postpone talking with their parents about housing options because such discussion has the potential to be unpleasant. It goes back to the changing parent-child relationship that we discussed earlier. All of a sudden, you're in a position where you feel you need to help your parents make decisions, instead of them helping you.

What you should realize, however, is that many people—older or not—welcome advice and help from family members. Sure, we all want to be in charge of our decisions, but sometimes a little guidance from someone you trust is a great help.

Maybe Mom and Dad have each been worrying about where they'll live when they can no longer keep up the big family home they've lived in for 35 years, but haven't even discussed it with each other. Mom might not want Dad to know how worried she gets when he climbs unsteadily onto a ladder to clean the windows. She's afraid he'll think that she doubts his ability to keep up with the work. Dad might think it will be too upsetting to Mom to have to talk about moving from the home she loves.

Out of what they each perceive as consideration for the other, or, because they simply don't know how to start the conversation, they don't talk about it at all. Having you initiate and open the discussion for them might be exactly what they need to start planning for the future.

Considering the Options

As stated earlier, senior citizens today have many options concerning where to live. There are innovative solutions, such as shared housing, or modular housing that can be moved onto your property or the property of another relative. There are continuing care communities where Mom and Dad can be assured they'll always have the care they need. There even is a new trend of foster care for adults, where Mom gets "adopted" by a foster family.

When you start looking for housing solutions, be sure that you consider the pros and cons of all the options, and consider factors such as your parents' health, their financial situation, their attitudes about where they'll live, how well they relate to other people, if they're willing to adhere to a schedule, and so forth. Talk to them about what housing solutions may be available in their area. Or, are they willing to move out of their community? Share your opinions about what sort of housing you think would work for them, and listen to their ideas and concerns.

Some housing alternatives just won't make sense for your parents. If Mom values her privacy above all else, it might be hard to ask her to move to an assisted living center where she has to share a room and a bathroom with a stranger. Many people don't like having to eat at certain times each day, as in some senior apartments and assisted living centers. Deciding where to live is difficult for anyone, and especially so for older people who are leaving their homes of many years, their neighborhoods, and often their support systems. Financial considerations will help determine where your folks will live.

Whose Decision Is It?

Some people like to be told what to do. They're uncomfortable deciding on their own, and actually appreciate it when a friend or family member makes important—or even non-important—decisions for them.

Most people, however, like to feel that they have control over their own lives and their situations, including where they live. Unless your parent is incompetent, or actually prefers that you make major decisions for her, let her decide where she'll live.

Beware of the parent who urges you to make important decisions for her, and then blames you when the situation doesn't work out the way she'd hoped. Some people avoid making decisions as a means of avoiding responsibility.

The problem, of course, is that you may feel very strongly that Mom's decision about where she'll live is wrong. She wants to renovate her home so that she can live there alone when she finishes the therapy she needed after suffering a stroke. You, on the other hand, are terrified to think of her being in the house by herself, even with the handrails that will have been installed in the hallways. She might fall. She might have another stroke. She might need help and not be able to get to the phone. Mom, however, insists that she'll be fine once she gets back to her own surroundings in her own home.

There are occasions when you and other family members are forced to make decisions for a parent, regardless of whether or not your input is welcome. If Mom's safety is at stake, or she's putting someone else in jeopardy, you need to step in and make sure she gets to a place where she'll be safe. If she can't remember to turn off the stove when she's finished using it, or she wanders out of the house and gets lost, or she essentially lives in one tiny room because she can't get up or down the stairs, you need to get her to a place where she'll get the help she needs in order to be safe.

Keeping Their Best Interests in Mind

When you're wrestling with Mom and Dad's living arrangement, it's vitally important to put their interests first. Sure, it would be great to have Mom move in to that little place right around the corner. The kids could walk over and spend some time with her whenever they wanted to. You could stop by and say hello on your way home from work, and it would be so convenient to pick up some groceries for her and drop them off on your way back from the store.

If Mom's lived in another state for her entire life, however, you need to think about whether she'll be happy in your neighborhood. She'd have to leave the house she shared with your dad before he died—the place where they lived happily for nearly all of their married lives.

Maybe you're pushing Mom and Dad to move to a continuing care retirement community you've been reading about. You're sure they'd be happy there because Dad could play golf and Mom could have her own plot in the community garden. They could enjoy the activities offered and have a great social life. In addition, it would really be a load off your mind, knowing that they'll receive whatever care is necessary for the rest of their lives.

Sounds great, doesn't it? Mom and Dad might think so too, but they're already worried about their financial situation, and continuing care communities normally are very expensive. To move to one would really strap them financially, leaving them with no money for travel or the other activities they enjoy.

Maybe you've been urging Dad to move out of his house for a couple of years now. It's a lot bigger than he needs, and you're sure he must be lonely there since Mom died. Most of the older neighbors that he knew have moved out, and the neighborhood is filling up with young families. You're sure he'd be happier in an apartment or condominium where he wouldn't have the worry of keeping up a house and property.

While your intentions are good, what you don't know is that Dad's gotten to be good friends with some of those young families that have moved in, and he's not lonely in the least. He loves to have the kids from next door stop by when they get home from school, and he's taken to filling his candy dish with special treats for them. He's found a great lawn service that takes care of his outside work, and the housekeeper that's worked for him for years still comes in twice a week. Dad is doing just fine on his own.

It's fine to make suggestions concerning your parents' living arrangements, but be sure you do so with their best interests fully in mind.

Staying Put

As much as you might like to see your folks safely situated in an assisted living facility or life care center, sometimes just staying where they are makes the most sense.

For many older people, the thought of moving is completely overwhelming. They have no idea what they'd do with all the belongings they've accumulated over 40 or 50 years. They don't like the thought of living among people they don't know. They greatly value their privacy and independence.

Mom's been living on her own for five years now since Dad died, and you and your siblings are worried that the house is getting to be too much for her. Mom, however, insists that she's fine, and can't imagine living anywhere else. She needs help with some chores every now and then, but she generally manages very well.

Should you insist that she leave her home? Would that be keeping her best interests in mind—or yours? Would you be imposing your wishes on her, regardless of what she wants? If Mom is able to manage, and it's important for her to remain in her house, she should stay. She will benefit psychologically and emotionally. If her house is mortgage free, it may make sense financially for her to stay.

If she's going to remain at home, your job is to help her make sure the house is as safe, comfortable, and as easy to maintain as possible.

Making the House Safe and Comfortable

If you and Mom (or Dad, of course, but we'll focus on Mom here since three-quarters of elderly people living by themselves are women) decide that your parent is going to stay at home, there are some measures you can take to assure that she'll be safe and comfortable. Many older people do better in their homes when some simple modifications are made. As people age, most experience failing eyesight. Most become less sure-footed. Some become forgetful. There are steps you can take to facilitate these changes and keep Mom safe and happy in her own home.

The National Resource Center on Supportive Housing and Home Modification, a group affiliated with the University of Southern California in Los Angeles, reports that the most common sources of accidental injury to elderly people in their homes are falls on stairway, floors, and in showers and bathtubs; burns or scalds from cooking or too-hot shower or bath water; and poisoning from medications. Fortunately, there are some easy measures you can take to prevent these kinds of accidents from happening to Mom.

Before we discuss how to prevent falls and burns, let's take a minute to think about the big picture. How old is Mom's house? How's the wiring? The plumbing? The insulation? Many older homes are in need of some repairs, and you (or Mom) may not even know it. If your parents always kept their home in tip-top condition, you may have nothing to worry about. But, what if Dad was sick for a while before he died and couldn't take care of things the way he always had?

If you suspect there may be some problems, don't hesitate to bring in a contractor or inspector to check things out. Maybe you've noticed some stains on the ceilings, indicating water damage from a leak in the roof or from an upstairs pipe. Or, you're unsure if the old electrical system can support all the extra appliances your parents have accumulated. It really is better to be safe than sorry. Find yourself a reputable plumber, electrician, roofer, or whoever your need, and have them check for problems. Take a look around for wires that might be frayed, or held together with tape. Check to make sure the outlets aren't overloaded. The bathroom and kitchen outlets should have circuit interrupters to prevent shocks from occurring. Look for faucets that drip, or are difficult to turn on and off. Once you've looked at the big picture, you can focus in on specific safety issues.

Preventing Falls

Many older people fall, and many more are afraid of falling, with good reason. Older bones break more easily than younger ones. Older skin is thinner and cuts and bruises more easily. And, more problems, such as bedsores and pneumonia, can occur while Mom's in bed healing from a bad fall. About 12,000 Americans die as a result of falls each year—most of them are elderly. And, falls cause more than 250,000 broken hips in the United States each year, 90 percent of them in people 65 or older, according to the American Academy of Orthopedic Surgeons. The key, of course, is preventing falls from occurring in the first place.

The most common falls occur on the steps, which, as you might imagine, can be very dangerous. If Mom has a history of falling, or if she's very unsteady on the stairs, it may be best to try to keep her away from them. Would she consider making a downstairs den into a bedroom so that she wouldn't have to be up and down the stairs? Could you afford to install a lift to carry her up and down the steps?

You can find out about stair lifts by checking the Yellow Pages under "Medical Equipment" or by searching the Internet. There's a great site called The Boulevard Abilities Mall that offers all kinds of adaptive devices meant to make life easier for elderly and disabled persons. It's a good place to check out, just to see what's available. You can find it at www.blvd.com.

If you can't avoid stairs, be sure every flight is equipped with a strong handrail she can hang onto. Ideally, handrails should be on both sides of the stairs, and should fully extend from top to bottom. Be especially attentive to stairs leading to a basement, and don't forget the outside stairs, as well. If Mom still goes up and down the cellar steps to do laundry or transport items, install a laundry shoot so she doesn't have to carry a basket down the stairs with her. Steps leading into the basement in older homes can be very steep.

Make sure all the steps have rubber treads for surer footing, and remember that carpeted stairs can be hazardous because the carpet makes it more difficult to see the edge of the step. Put bright-colored tape along the edge of each step so Mom can clearly see where it ends.

Falls occur most frequently on stairs, but they also occur in other areas of the home. Frequent culprits in causing these falls are throw rugs and worn, uneven carpeting. Many people keep a small rug in front of a door for wiping dirty shoes. If Mom's house has a cement basement floor, chances are she has several rugs there to stand on as she does chores. These rugs could be removed entirely, or at the very least secured with rubber backing so they don't slide. Even with rubber backing, however, they still can be a tripping hazard.

Your goal should be to make the areas where Mom walks as level as possible. Try to eliminate anything that sticks up, or could otherwise get in her way, and make sure she has clear vision of the areas in which she walks.

- Move any small benches, plant pots, waste cans, or other small items out of the walking areas. Watch for furniture legs that curve outward, causing a possible tripping hazard.
- Make sure no wires are stretched across the floor where she walks.
- Install handrails in the hallways.
- Avoid thick-pile carpets that can snag a heel or toe.
- Put nightlights along any routes Mom might travel at night, such as those leading to the kitchen or bathroom.
- Leave a small light turned on at night in the bathroom or kitchen if chances are good that she'll be visiting.

- Avoid slippery floors, such as those that are heavily waxed or prone to getting wet. Clean up spills immediately after they occur.

Bathrooms are a common place for falls, due mostly to slipping while getting in or out of the bathtub or shower. You can minimize Mom's chances of falling in the bathroom by putting grab bars near the tub and toilet. Get a raised toilet seat, which makes it much easier to get up and down.

The tub and shower should have rubber strips or a rubber mat to prevent Mom from slipping. If she has trouble getting up and down in the bathtub, or standing long enough to shower, get a stool or chair designed for that use. Mom can sit in the chair while she showers, or use a shower hose to wash herself. Bar soap is slippery and easy to drop in the shower. Install a liquid-soap dispenser on the wall inside the shower. Tell her to be extremely careful when using any sort of bath oil or soap that might make the tub or shower slippery.

Make sure there's a bar for her to hold onto as she steps out of the tub. If she's using a towel rack for this purpose, make sure it's securely fastened. They sometimes pull out of the wall. And, make sure to have rubber-backed rugs or mats on the bathroom floor to prevent her from slipping on wet tile.

Some general steps you can take to help keep Mom from falling include:
- Make sure she has sturdy, non-slip shoes. Some women who have worn high heels all their lives are reluctant to give them up, but flat shoes with a wide base make for much safer walking. Warn Mom not to walk around the house wearing only socks, which can be slippery, and make sure her bedroom slippers have non-slip soles.
- Remove any furniture that's on wheels or rollers. The last thing Mom needs is a chair that will fly out from under her when she stands up.
- Locate phones where Mom can reach them easily, or get her a cordless phone that she can sit next to her favorite chair.
- Make sure she has something sturdy to hold onto when she's getting dressed.
- Make sure the kitchen equipment that she uses frequently is within her reach. Same goes for plants that need to be watered, books, and so forth. Ask her to avoid climbing onto stepladders or benches to reach such items.
- If Mom lives in an area that gets snow and ice, be sure she's extra careful when walking outside in the winter. Keep a bucket of salt by the front door so she can throw out a handful onto ice before leaving the house. Make sure she has rubber boots to wear.

Preventing Burns

Next to falls, burns are one of the most common household injuries among elderly people. Most burns occur in two areas of the house—the kitchen and the bathroom.

The kitchen is easy to figure. There are lots of burn hazards when cooking. The main cause of burns in the bathroom is from overly hot water in the shower or tub. Older skin is thinner than younger skin and it burns more easily, but most older people don't realize this until they've suffered an injury.

This can easily be avoided by resetting the water heater so that the water temperature can't get above 120 degrees. This is plenty warm for washing dishes and keeping things clean, but it won't burn Mom's skin.

In the kitchen, make sure Mom has good, thick potholders or oven mitts to use when cooking. If these aren't handy, she's likely to use a towel to pull a pot off the stove, risking the possibility that it will get against the burner and catch on fire. If Mom doesn't have a microwave, consider buying her one or urging her to buy one. Remember, though, that items coming out of a microwave can be extremely hot.

Make sure there is a plan for getting out of the house in case of a fire. Call the local fire company and ask if they have a sign you can place on her bedroom window to alert firefighters that an elderly person may be in that room if a fire should occur.

If she has trouble seeing knobs and dials, you can buy new ones with large numbers and letters to make them easier for her to read. The Abilities Mall, mentioned earlier in this chapter, has a good selection of such items.

Older people generally like their homes to be a bit warmer than younger ones. Some try to cut down on heating bills by using space heaters or building fires in a fireplace. Some types of space heaters can be very dangerous if they're placed too near a piece of furniture, and others can cause poisonous fumes. Fireplaces are cozy, but building a fire is a lot of work, and needs careful monitoring to be safe. Ask Mom to save the fireplace until you're over to share it with her. If she's always cold, buy her some comfy long underwear, a heavy sweater, maybe a shawl.

Preventing Accidental Poisoning

Many people, both young and old, have trouble keeping track of their medicines. Keeping up with daily medications can be a big problem for an older person, especially one who's become a bit forgetful or is suffering from the early stages of dementia. Failing eyesight also can make it difficult to get the right pills in the right dosages. It's not unusual for an elderly person to experience severe side effects from taking too much medication, and every year thousands of people—many of them elderly—are hospitalized due to accidental poisoning.

A pill organizer can be a great help to someone who has to take several medications each day. Available at the pharmacy, you can keep a week's worth of pills in them, divided in up to four doses every day. Try to help her, or have somebody else help her to fill the organizer each week.

Another place to watch for accidental poisoning is Mom's kitchen. Some people hang on to food that should have been thrown out, or not cook potentially dangerous foods such as poultry or eggs thoroughly enough. Poor eyesight also might make it difficult to keep the kitchen clean, resulting in unsanitary conditions that may lead to food-related illness.

All these safety warnings aren't meant to scare you, or your parent. And, accidents can happen anywhere, not only in Mom's house. This section is only intended to make you more aware of potential risks, and get you thinking about how to keep Mom as safe as possible. A few other suggestions include:

- If Mom loves her independence, but worries about needing help and not being able to get to the phone, consider getting her a medical alert system for her home. This is a device Mom wears around her neck or wrist. If she falls, or is suddenly very ill, she can press the button that sends a message to an emergency response center. Some of these systems are for sale, while others can be rented.
- See that Mom has good outside lights, and that her path is clearly illuminated when she comes in at night. If she puts her car in a garage, she should have an electric garage door opener so she can drive right in and close the door behind her without leaving the car.
- Make sure that a close neighbor or two have your phone number, or the number of a friend or relative who lives close to Mom.
- You don't want to be overly protective or domineering, but it's a good idea to check in with Mom every day. If you have siblings, you could arrange a schedule so that one of you calls each day.

Learning What Services and Help are Available

If Mom is going to stay at home, you don't have to carry the load of helping her all by yourself. There are many community services aimed at the elderly, and private companies designed to assist elderly people are becoming more popular all the time.

A good place to start is with the area agency on aging. Workers there should be able to tell you what's available in the community in the way of home helpers, meal-delivery programs, drop-in visitors, transportation services, and senior centers.

Just because Mom wants to stay in her own house, it doesn't mean she wants to be alone all the time. Many communities have groups whose members volunteer to check in with an elderly person by telephone every day or two, or stop by for a visit once a week. There may be volunteers to take Mom to the grocery store or the doctor's office. Remember, too, that some grocery stores deliver to elderly customers. Senior centers offer wonderful social opportunities, and many provide a hot lunch or dinner.

Loneliness is a potential problem for elderly people who live alone. It's important that Mom keeps up with friends and remains as active as she can. Many older people don't like to ask for help for fear of being a bother to a friend or relative.

If she's having trouble getting meals together, you may be able to arrange for Meals-on-Wheels or another meal delivery program. Check with Mom's church or synagogue to see what kind of programs they have that are designed for elderly people. Many have groups that meet once or twice a month, and most houses of worship can arrange for visitors to stop by Mom's house now and then.

You might have to look around a bit to find out what sort of help is available for Mom in the community, but it's out there. Start with the government pages in the phone book (those are the blue pages), and don't forget to contact the area United Way for a directory of community resources.

Financial Considerations of Staying at Home

We've spent a lot of time discussing how to keep Mom (or Dad) safe and comfortable at home. Now, we've got to look at keeping her financially comfortable at home. In fact, finances will be a big factor in whether or not it makes sense for Mom to stay at home or move to another sort of living arrangement.

If her house is paid for and in good condition, it may be less expensive for her to continue living there than to move to an apartment or assisted living. Of course, she'll need to continue paying property taxes as long as she lives at home, and there are expenses associated with maintenance.

If Mom is having trouble taking care of her personal needs, you may need to look for home-care assistance, which provides services such as laundry, cooking, helping with bathing and dressing, running errands, some housekeeping, and so forth. This type of service can run anywhere from about $10 to $30 an hour, although some communities have services that operate on a sliding fee. The area agency on aging should have information about this type of service

A growing trend among the elderly is shared housing. Let's face it. There are a lot of elderly people out there in pretty much the same boat. Many have lost a spouse, and are still living in their family homes—alone. Others have moved to a smaller home or an apartment, and find that they're lonely. Having someone move in to share expenses and provide companionship might be a great solution to Mom's financial worries, assure that she won't be lonely, and provide a source of help if she needs it.

Some elder-roomies are people who have known each other for years, while other are together only because each was looking to share housing. Regardless, Mom should be very specific about what she expects from a housemate. Issues such as smoking, visitors, cooking, shopping, and privacy all should be addressed before an agreement is completed.

Take a few minutes to review home equity conversion plans, such as reverse mortgages. They may be a source of income to allow Mom to stay put. Staying in their own home may often be the best solution for your parent or parents. Sometimes, however, it becomes impossible, and you know they've got to move.

Moving Out

Even when everyone concedes that moving out is the best thing to do, it can be a wrenching experience. About a year after my father died, my mother moved from the house in which we'd grown up. Even though we all agreed that it was for the best, walking around those quiet, empty rooms for the last time was very, very sad. If Mom or Dad is moving against her or his will, it's even worse.

As much as you might love to have Mom go on living in the family home, there are occasions when it becomes clear it's just not possible.

Knowing when it's time for an aging parent to move out of her own home into a different living arrangement is a judgment call, but sometimes it becomes very obvious.

- If her safety, or the safety of someone else in the home is at stake, she should move.
- If she simply can't take care of herself, despite help that you've arranged for her, she should move.
- If you've looked at all the options and it's clear that she can't handle the expenses of keeping the house, she should move.
- If she's become depressed and withdrawn because she's alone for the great majority of the time, she should move.
- If she is isolated by her location and can no longer drive, she should move.
- If taking care of her in her home has become absolutely more than you, as her primary caregiver can do, she should move.

Ideally, Mom will get out of her house and into a more manageable situation before it becomes absolutely necessary. That way, she can take some time to consider her options and decide what arrangement makes the most sense for her.

Often, however, a person is forced to leave her home suddenly following a stroke, an illness, or an accident. It becomes clear soon after that she won't be able to return to the house, and you're stuck scrambling around to find a place for her to live.

If you're an only child, you'll probably bear much of the responsibility for Mom's move. If you have brothers and sisters, urge everyone to get involved, both with planning and the actual move. Family members all should feel free to express their opinions on where Mom should live. But if your mother is capable of making the decision, she should have the final say.

Helping Mom Put the House Up For Sale

Once Mom has decided to move, you'll need to find a good realtor to handle the sale. It's not advisable to try to sell Mom's house by yourself, unless you're very knowledgeable about the ins and outs of real estate. And, you'd have to make sure that you, or another family member or friend, could be at the house every time someone wanted to look at it. Don't ever leave an elderly parent to show a house to a stranger by herself.

Most realtors require you to sign a contract stating that you'll work with them for a specified period of time (usually six months). If the contract expires and you're not happy with the realtor's work, don't feel obligated to extend the contract. You're perfectly within your rights to look for someone else to handle the sale of the house.

If the same realtor has sold six houses in Mom's neighborhood in the past four months, give him a call. He already knows the neighborhood, and may know of people interested in buying in the area. When hiring a realtor, always consider his experience, and don't be afraid to ask for referrals from other clients.

RE/MAX realtors, which has more than 4,000 offices worldwide, lists 20 suggestions to improve your chances of selling a house. They're listed below.

- Make the most of a first impression. A well-manicured lawn, neatly trimmed shrubs and a clutter-free porch welcome prospects. So does a freshly painted—or at least freshly scrubbed—front door. If it's autumn, rake the leaves. If it's winter, shovel the walkways.
- Invest a few hours for future dividends. Clean up the living room, bathroom, and kitchen. If the woodwork is scuffed or the paint is fading, consider some minor redecoration. Fresh wallpaper adds charm and value to the property. If you don't have the time, think about hiring someone.
- Check faucets and bulbs. Dripping water rattles the nerves, discolors sinks, and suggests faulty or worn-out plumbing. Burned-out bulbs or faulty wiring leave prospects in the dark. Don't let little problems detract from what's right with the home.
- Don't shut out a sale. If cabinets or closet doors stick in the home, you can be sure they will also stick in a prospect's mind. Make sure drawers, closets, and cabinets open and close smoothly.
- Think safety. Be aware of possible safety hazards, such as throw rugs or rickety handrails. Make the residence as non-perilous as possible for visitors.
- Make room for space. Remember, potential buyers are looking for more than just comfortable living space. They're looking for storage space, too. Make sure the attic and basement are clean and free of unnecessary items.
- Consider the closets. The better organized a closet, the larger it appears. Now's the time to box up those unwanted clothes and donate them to charity.

- Make the bathroom sparkle. Bathrooms sell homes, so let them shine. Check and repair damaged or unsightly caulking in the tubs and showers. Display the best towels, mats, and shower curtains.
- Create dream bedrooms. Make the rooms look spacious by getting rid of excess furniture, and display cheerful bedspreads and curtains.
- Open up in the daytime. Let prospective buyers see how bright and cheery the house is by opening the curtains and drapes.
- Lighten up at night. Turn on a lot of lights—both inside and out—when showing the house at night. Lights add color and warmth, and make prospects feel welcome.
- Avoid crowd scenes. Potential buyers often feel like intruders when they enter a home filled with people. Rather than giving the house the attention it deserves, they're likely to hurry through. Keep the number of people present to a minimum.
- Watch your pets. Dogs and cats are great companions, but not when you're showing your home. Remove pets from the house while it's being shown.
- Think volume. Rock-and-roll will never die, but it might kill a real estate transaction. Turn the stereo and TV off, or at least down when showing the house.
- Relax. Be friendly, but don't try to force conversation. Prospects want to view your home with a minimum of distraction.
- Don't apologize. Regardless of how humble the house is, never apologize for its shortcomings. If a prospect volunteers a derogatory comment about the home's appearance, let your real estate agent handle the situation.
- Keep a low profile. Nobody knows the home as well as you do, but your realtor know buyers—what they need and what they want. Your realtor will have an easier time articulating the virtues of your home if you stay in the background.
- Don't turn the home into a second-hand store. When prospects come to view the home, don't distract them with offers to sell the furnishings you no longer need. You may lose the biggest sale of all.
- Defer to experience. When prospects want to talk price, terms, or other real estate matters, let them speak to your realtor. Don't negotiate directly with a prospective buyer.
- Help your agent. Your realtor will have an easier time selling the home if showings are scheduled through his or her office. Don't arrange directly for prospective buyers to come to the home.

Moving—What to Take and What to Leave

Packing up 40 years worth of belongings is not an easy task. Neither is helping your parent decide what he should take to his or her new home, and what they'll no longer need. Be realistic when deciding what furniture to take along. Mom is probably moving to a much smaller place, and it's easy to overestimate how much furniture will fit.

Encourage Mom to take possessions that are important to her, such as photographs and items that were handed down from other family members. Try to discourage her, however, from taking along every piece of Tupperware she owns, five-year's worth of phone books, or the extra set of glasses that are chipped and cracked.

Moving is an overwhelming job for many elderly people, and Mom is likely to need help. The most difficult part of getting her moved will not be wrapping dishes and putting them in boxes. It will be deciding what to keep. You may have to go around the house with her and assess nearly every item to determine if it will go or stay.

If there are items she really wants to keep, but there won't be room in her new home, offer to store them in a safe place. If there's no room in Mom's new apartment to store the 50 photo albums she's compiled over the years, for instance, offer to put them in boxes and store them in your basement. Then, take a couple to her at a time to look through. Just knowing that her possessions are someplace where she can get them may be a great comfort.

If there is a lot of furniture and other items left in house, you can contact an auctioneer or dealer about buying it. An auctioneer usually agrees to take and sell certain items, and will give you a percentage of what he gets. A dealer probably would make you an outright offer for the items he wants. There also are people who will come in after a move and take out everything that's left in the house. They sometimes will pay you a minimal amount for what they take, or, you may have to pay them to take it. They'll sometimes trade their services for the items they take.

Emotional Considerations

Keep in mind that the moving period will be a very emotional time for everyone, but especially for your elderly parent. She'll probably be working harder than normal to prepare for the move, and may be very tired. She may experience some depression related to the move.

Mom may be extremely anxious and nervous as she prepares to leave the home in which she's comfortable to move into a place she doesn't know. If she's moving into an assisted living facility, she may feel that she's about to lose her independence. Remember that a home is a lot more than just a house.

Try to take a little extra care of Mom during this time, and enlist help from siblings, friends, or other relatives when possible. If you don't live close by, try to arrange for someone who does to help her. Make sure that Mom eats properly, gets enough sleep, and continues to take whatever medications may have been prescribed for her. Assure her that she'll have plenty of help, and don't minimize her concerns associated with moving. Try to be as patient with her as you can, and remember that life will eventually return to normal.

You might wonder if you've done the right thing regarding Mom's housing situation, whether she stays at home, or moves somewhere else. It's natural to worry about aging parents, and to have doubts concerning the decisions you help them to make. Assure yourself that you've done your best, and trust that whatever situation you've chosen for Mom probably will work out just fine.

Checklist to Assure Safety of Older People Living at Home

The most common sources of injury to elderly people in their own homes, according to the National Resource Center on Supportive Housing and Home Modification, are falls, burns, and poisoning.

A checklist is provided below to help you determine how safe your parent or parents may be in their home.

To Prevent Falls from Occurring:

Are the stairs covered with a non-slip surface? _____

If stairs are carpeted, is there a colored strip at the edge of each one to make it easier to determine the edge of the step? _____

Do you worry about your parent using the stairs? _____

Could arrangements be made to avoid or minimize the use of stairs (move a bedroom downstairs or a washer upstairs, etc.)? _____

Have you considered a chair lift as a means of getting up and down steps?

_____

Does each flight of stairs have a strong, sturdy handrail—preferably on both sides? _____

Have all throw rugs and other possible fall hazards been removed from traffic areas? _____

Are there handrails in the hallways and in other frequently traveled areas?

_____

Have all wires been taped along the walls to eliminate a tripping hazard?

_____

Are there nightlights turned on at night so your parent can see in dark areas?

_____

Have grab bars been installed in the tub and around the toilet to minimize the chance of a fall there? _____

Does the shower or bath have rubber strips or a rubber mat so that it's not slippery? _____

Are bathroom rugs non-slip and well secured? _____

Does your parent wear sturdy, non-slip shoes rather than slippery slippers or socks? _____

Is there a bar for your parent to hold onto while getting dressed? _____

Are plants, kitchen items, etc. easily accessible to prevent your parent from having to reach or climb on something to get them? _____

Have you arranged to have snow and ice removed to prevent slippery conditions? _____

Is there sufficient outside lighting to light the way when your parent enters the house at night? _____

To Prevent Burns from Occurring:

Is the water heat set so that water temperature can't get above 120 degrees?

_____

Are there plenty of thick potholders or oven mitts available in the kitchen?

_____

Is there a plan in place for leaving the house in the event of a fire? _____

Are there enough smoke alarms in the house, and are the batteries checked regularly? _____

Is the house free of portable heaters or space heaters that could start a fire?

_____

Is there a microwave available for use instead of the stove or oven? _____

Is your parent careful to turn off all electrical appliances when not in use?

_____

To Prevent Accidental Poisoning from Occurring:

Are your parent's medications sorted into a pill organizer, making it easy for him or her to keep track of doses? _____

Does your parent read, understand, and follow instructions when taking his or her medications? _____

Does your parent get prescriptions for medicines from more than one doctor?

_____

If so, does each doctor know the other medicines that your parent is taking?

_____

Is your parent aware of possible problems caused by mixing certain types of medications? _____

Is your parent's house reasonably clean, especially in the kitchen? _____

Does your parent practice sanitary thawing, cooking, and food storage methods? _____

Does your parent have access to fresh, healthy foods on a regular basis?

_____

General Precautions to Keep Your Parent Safe:

Does someone check in with your elderly parent on a regular basis? _____

Does your parent have a list of numbers to call in case of an emergency?

_____

Nursing Home Checklist

The Department of Health and Human Services recommends that you use this checklist when visiting a nursing home you may be considering for a parent, other relative, or friend. Fill out a checklist for each home you visit, and them compare the lists.

General Questions:

Is the facility Medicare certified? _____

Is the facility Medicaid certified? _____

Is the facility currently accepting new patients? _____

What is the waiting period for admission? _____

How many beds are available in the level of care your parent needs?

_____

Nursing Home Questions:

Are the home and current administrator licensed by the state? _____

Does the home conduct background checks on all staff members? _____

Does the home have special service units, such as an Alzheimer's wing?

_____

Does the home provide abuse protection training? _____

Does the home have procedures in place to safeguard patient's possessions?

_____

Quality of Life Questions:

Do residents have choices or options concerning their daily routines? _____

Is the interaction between staff and patients warm and friendly? _____

Is the home easy for friends and family to visit? _____

Does the nursing home meet your cultural, religious, or language needs?

_____

Does the home smell and look clean? _____

Is the home kept at a comfortable temperature? _____

Are residents permitted to have personal items and furniture in their rooms?

_____

Are the common rooms and resident rooms comfortable and clean?

_____

Are the living and dining areas kept fairly quiet? _____

Can residents choose activities, such as games or crafts, in which to participate? _____

Are residents permitted and encouraged to go outdoors when applicable?

_____

Does the home have outside volunteer participation? _____

Quality of Care Questions:

Has the facility corrected any deficiencies that showed up in the state inspection? _____

Do residents continue to see their personal care physicians? _____

Do residents appear to be clean, appropriately dressed and well groomed?

_____

Does staff respond quickly to calls for help? _____

Do the administrator and staff seem comfortable with each other and with patients? _____

Do residents have the same caregivers on a regular basis? _____

Is there sufficient staff available on nights and weekends, as well as during the day? _____

Does the home have an arrangement for emergency situations with an area hospital? _____

Are family members encouraged and able to attend care-plan meetings with staff? _____

Nutrition and Hydration Questions:

Is there enough staff to assist any residents who need help with eating?

_____

Does the food look and smell good, and is offered at proper temperatures?

_____

Do residents have a choice of food at each meal? _____

Do residents have water available in their rooms at all times? _____

Does staff monitor residents' weights? _____

Are residents encouraged to drink if not able to do so on their own? _____

Are there nutritious snacks available between meals? _____

Is the dining room a pleasant, friendly place? _____

Safety Questions:

Are there handrails in the hallways and grab bars in the bathrooms?

_____

Are all exits clearly marked? _____

Are hallways well lighted and free of clutter? _____

Are spills and other accidents cleaned up quickly? _____

Does the home have working smoke detectors, alarms, and sprinkler systems?

_____

Is there adequate staff to assist residents in the event of an emergency?

_____

Is a clear evacuation plan in place? _____

Chapter Seven

Housing Options

If your parents have decided to move, but don't know where they want to go, you can help them by letting them know of all the options that are available. While senior housing used to be pretty limited—and a lot of it was pretty dismal—the situation definitely has changed for the better.

Gertrude, a 92-year-old friend, sold a large home and moved with her husband about four years ago to an apartment in what's called a retirement residence. Bill has since died, but Gertrude continues to live in the spacious apartment. Although she has a small kitchen with a microwave and a refrigerator, she eats all her meals downstairs in a beautiful dining room, complete with waiters and waitresses and a choice of entrees. Her monthly fee includes all meals, laundry service for sheets and towels, and light housecleaning. If she gets sick, residence staff will deliver food to her apartment.

Gertrude plays bridge several times a week with other women who live in the building, and sometimes attends lectures and programs in the activity room. Because she doesn't drive, it's convenient that a hairdresser comes to the building at regular intervals, and there's a drug store and other shops within walking distance. The residence also has a van used to transport residents to area stores and doctors' offices. She can visit the in-house library, or sit by a fireplace in one of the common areas. Or, she can stay in her own apartment, entertaining guests or just spending time alone.

Another elderly friend, Peg, lives in a continuing care retirement community. Peg paid an entrance fee that got her a nice apartment, and she pays a monthly fee to stay there. The agreement she signed when she moved in states that Peg will live independently in her apartment for as long as she's able. If the time comes that she's no longer able to be in her apartment, the facility will sell her apartment, and assisted living or skilled nursing care will be provided for as long as Peg lives.

At age 88, Peg still lives in her own apartment, but she now has meals delivered to her door instead of walking the distance to the dining room. Her eyesight is failing rapidly, and she's thinking about making the move to the facility's assisted living area. Residents in the assisted living area have their own dining room, and there's help available for dressing, making beds, and so forth. If she's ever unable to get along in the assisted living area, she'll be moved into the community's skilled nursing facility, which is essentially a nursing home. Knowing that she'll be taken care of is great comfort to Peg.

My mother-in-law, Helen, moved recently from her three-story house to a one-floor condominium that's very close to our house. At age 76, Helen still works part time, drives, does her own cooking and cleaning, and is generally in good health. Moving to the condo now, instead of waiting until she's forced to make a move, gives her, and my husband and me, the peace of mind that she'll be in a manageable housing situation if it should become more difficult for her to get around. There are no steps to worry about, her outside maintenance is all taken care of, and she's close enough for us to check on her every day, if that would be necessary.

My best friend, Joanie, moved from Pennsylvania to Florida 20 years ago when she married Amos. When they built a new home, they included space for an apartment, but left it unfinished. When Joanie's parents sold their home in Pennsylvania, she and Amos had the apartment finished and invited Jack and Jean to use it. Jean is in her late 70s and Jack in his early 80s. It's not a perfect situation, but they all try hard to make it work. Jack helps with yard work and the two dogs, while Jean keeps an eye on Emma, her 12-year-old granddaughter. Joanie is adamant that she'll have her parents live with her for as long as it's in any way possible, and Jack and Jean enjoy being around Joanie, Amos, Emma, and their friends.

These four situations are intended to give you (and your parents) an idea of some of the options available. In this chapter, we'll examine more options for living arrangements for elderly parents, starting with having them move in with you.

Should Your Parents Move In With You?

If you asked my friend Joanie the question just above, her answer would vary from a resounding "yes" to a doubtful "probably not," depending on the day you asked and what happened to be going on at the time.

Having your parents, or a parent move in to your home can be extremely difficult. It also can be very rewarding. My sister-in-law and brother had her parents live with them for almost three years until their deaths, which were just two months apart. Julia still wonders, eight years later, if she could have done more for them. She still has occasional misgivings about things that happened—or didn't happen. She also has the satisfaction, however, of knowing she made the last months of her parents' lives as comfortable and secure as possible. And, she's happy for the time they had together before her parents died.

Whether your parents should move in with you is an important decision, and certainly one that should not be made lightly. For many people, wanting to have your parents with you if they're sick or unable to get along on their own is a natural reaction. You want to take care of them, because they took care of you. But, before you hang out the "Welcome Mom and Dad" sign, there are some things you should think about very carefully.

- The nature of your relationship. Do you and your parents (or parent) have an amicable relationship that's based on mutual respect? Or do you drive each other crazy every time you're together for more than a couple of hours? Will Dad respect the fact that it's your home and you make the decisions regarding it and what goes on in it? Or will he revert back to the good old days when he got to tell you what to do and make important decisions for you? Will he be resentful because he's living with your and no longer in his own home?

- The nature of your parents' relationship with the rest of your family. If it was just you and your parents, you could decide on your own whether or not they should live with you. If you have a spouse or other partner, and children of your own, however, the decision is a bit more involved. Does your mother get along with your wife, or does she criticize everything she does? Does it drive your father nuts when your kids play loud music or have their friends over? If so, you'd better think twice about having the folks move in.

- Your living space. If you live in a tiny, two-bedroom apartment with your husband, two kids, and a Golden Retriever, asking your parents move in is just plain crazy. Where will they sleep—under the kitchen sink? Even if you have a big house, you need to think about whether there's space that will work for Mom and Dad. If the third floor is empty, but they can't climb the steps to get there, the space is useless to them. On the other hand, if you have a den or office that doesn't get much use, it might be perfect space for your parents.

- Your financial situation. If Mom's run out of money, or won't have any money until she sells her house, will you be able to support her in the meantime? Do you have siblings that could contribute financially to her care? Consider additional expenses that will occur from having her in the house—increased water and heating bills, groceries, medicines, and so forth.
- Your other obligations. Do you have a full-time job? Lots of commitments at your kids' schools? Frequent night meetings at your church or synagogue? Do you already feel like there's not enough time to do everything you need to do? Remember that having an extra person (or two) in your home is an added responsibility. Maybe you'll be really lucky and Mom will cook dinner every night, do all the laundry and ironing, and bake cookies for the kids on Saturdays. If she is ill and needs substantial care, however, she'll be more of an obligation than a help.
- Are you equipped to care for him? If Dad has cancer and has been given nine months to live, will you realistically be able to care for him as his condition progresses? You might have him move in with you temporarily, with the understanding that when you can no longer care for him, he'll go to a skilled nursing center or hospice care. Be up front with him about your capabilities and limitations. Assure him that you'll do everything you can for him, but remind him that you're not a nurse, and your ability to care for him is limited.

These are just some of the topics you should think about when deciding whether or not to invite Mom and Dad to move in. You probably can come up with many more that pertain to your own situation. If, after careful consideration, your parents move in, make sure you establish some ground rules right from the start, and that everyone understands them. Some rules to consider include the following:
- It's your home, and your parents need to respect you and your spouse as the primary decision-makers.
- You need to respect and adapt to each other's routines, habits, and schedules. If Mom likes to have a cup of tea every day at 4 p.m. and has done so for 30 years, don't tell her she can't use the kitchen at that time because the kids are getting an after-school snack. If you like to have friends over for dinner on Saturday nights, Mom should agree to eat

early that night and find something to do elsewhere in the house, if that's what you wish. If Dad gets up every morning at 6 and you like to sleep until 9 on Saturdays, he should agree to be as quiet as possible until you're awake.

- If they're able, your parents should be expected to help with some household chores, such as taking out trash, washing dishes, or folding laundry.
- Let Dad know that it's not your job to entertain him. Tell Dad you won't be available for checkers every night after dinner, just because you always played when you visited him in his own home. Do, however, make time to have a game with him every now and then.
- Be patient and adaptable. A new living arrangement will be an adjustment for everyone. Don't be discouraged if the situation doesn't seem ideal right away, as it may take some time for everyone to get comfortable.
- Listen to each other and take action when necessary, but stay out of the middle as much as possible. If your 15-year-old son is upset because Grandma goes into his room every day to make the bed and sort the clothing in his drawers, listen carefully when he tells you how he feels, and be sympathetic. Be supportive and help him if necessary, but try to stay out of the middle.
- Know when to say "no more." If the living arrangement turns out to be a disaster, do something about it. Don't sacrifice your marriage, your relationship with your kids, or your relationship with your parents because you're too proud or stubborn to admit you've made a mistake by having your parent come to live with you. Present your parents with some other living alternatives and help them to get comfortably situated somewhere else.

If having your parents live in your house isn't an option due to space or other reasons, there may be some alternatives to consider.

ECHO Housing

ECHO homes (it stands for Elder Cottage Housing Opportunity) are fairly new, but they're gaining in popularity. They're modular homes that you move onto your property for as long as necessary, and remove them when they're no longer needed.

To learn more about ECHO housing, go to Senior Resource's website at www.seniorresouce.com/hecho.htm. You can read all about this innovative housing alternative, including ideas for financing.

Usually about the size of a large garage, a typical ECHO home includes a living room, kitchen, eating area, bathroom, and one or two bedrooms. Because they're designed especially for older people, they are wheel chair accessible, energy efficient, and all on one level. They typically cost about $25,000. Be sure to check with the municipality in which you live to make sure this type of housing is permitted.

In–Law Apartments

If you think your parent or parents might be with you for quite a while, you might consider adding space onto your house. In-law, or accessory apartments, typically contain a living area, bedroom, bathroom, and may, or may not, have a kitchen. Some families prefer that Mom eats with them instead of cooking her own food, while others prefer to cook and eat separately. Most in-law apartments have an entrance that's separate from the main part of the house.

People who have these types of apartments sometimes rent them to elderly people who are not related, rather than have the space go unused. If you know of one in your community or in Mom's community and you're looking for a place for Mom to live, it might be worth checking out.

These can be great because they allow for a lot more privacy than having your parents living in the main part of your home. The downside is that it's expensive to put an addition on your home. Also, consider how the space will be used once Mom no longer lives there. Again, be sure to check zoning regulations before deciding to add an in-law apartment onto your home.

Adult or Retirement Communities

If you and your parents have decided that living together just won't work, you'll need an alternative. One you can consider is a retirement community, sometimes called an adult community.

Retirement communities vary greatly in scope, and can mean different things to different people. Some retirement communities offer continuing care, and we'll discuss that concept a lot more in the next section. For now, however, we're talking about retirement communities that simply are places intended for older people.

Some retirement communities are open to people of any age (although hardly anyone who's not of retirement age moves in), while others specify that you must be over a certain age, usually somewhere between 55 and 65, in order to move in. Retirement communities vary in size and offerings, too.

Commonly, a retirement community contains small one-story homes on small lots. Outside maintenance usually is provided, although services vary from community to community. There normally are common areas for residents to share, and some communities include a lake or pond for fishing, a golf course, tennis courts, shuffleboard courts, horseshoe pits, and so forth. Many times there are planned activities, such as bingo or card games, day or overnight trips, entertainment, and educational programs. Retirement communities that contain single homes normally do not provide meals for residents, although some might have a restaurant or cafeteria on the campus.

Your parent would either buy or rent the house, and would pay a monthly or quarterly fee for services such as grass cutting, snow removal, and outside painting. There usually are rules that residents must agree to follow, such as no hanging laundry outside, no loud noise between 10 p.m. and 6 a.m., and so forth.

If your parents are considering moving to a retirement community, be sure they shop around before committing themselves. There are huge differences from community to community, and, while many are very nice, others are less desirable. The cost of retirement communities varies greatly depending on location, the type of homes, services provided, and whether your parent would buy or rent. Some retirement communities offer lots for sale, and allow you to build a house of your choice. There usually are restrictions on the building, however.

Continuing Care Retirement Communities

As explained earlier in this chapter, continuing care communities are those that offer independent living, assisted living, and skilled care, all on the same campus. They're usually upscale, large complexes, sometimes sprawling over miles of land.

Although it varies from community to community, the basic concept of a continuing care retirement community is as follows. Mom and Dad pay an entrance fee that, depending on how much they pay, gets them a house or an apartment. If your parents are considering a continuing care community, be sure to ask about the policy regarding ownership. In some communities, the entrance fee buys the house or apartment, while in others, the community continues to own the home in which your parents live.

Continuing care communities generally have very nice dining rooms, although if Mom and Dad have a kitchen and prefer not to eat in the common area, they're not required to. They generally offer many activities, such as golf, swimming, tennis, trips, music programs, and opportunity for gardening and woodworking. Most have on-site banking available, a library, beauty shop and barber, a drug store and pharmacy, and so forth.

Mom and Dad live independently until something happens that one of them can't. Let's say that Mom has a stroke. When she returns from the hospital, she and Dad find that she can't take care of herself, and it's too much for Dad to handle. At that point, Mom gets moved to the assisted living section of the community, while Dad remains in their apartment. Dad can go visit Mom every day, and has peace of mind knowing that she's getting the care she needs. If Mom gets well enough to take care of herself again, she moves back in with Dad. If she continues to need assistance, she stays where she is. And, if she encounters another health problem that makes her unable to do anything for herself, she'll be moved to the skilled care section of the facility, which is really a nursing home.

Advantages and Disadvantages of Continuing Care Communities

As mentioned earlier in this chapter, continuing care communities can be great for people who don't have children or other close family members. And, they also can provide peace of mind for those who don't want to become a burden on their families.

In addition, there are other advantages with this type of living. These communities typically attract active seniors who enjoy socializing and participating in different activities. They can provide a sense of community as people get to know each other, and many new friendships form in these places. There is plenty to do, but residents need to do only what they enjoy. There is no outside maintenance, leaving residents with abundant leisure time.

On the downside, some people who live in these types of communities complain that there are too many rules, or too many people, or too little service.

These communities usually are built fairly quickly, and there sometimes are questions about the quality of construction.

On a very serious note, these communities sometimes assume authority to decide what level of care their residents require. If that's the case, Mom or Dad could be refused entry into assisted living, even if they believe that he or she requires it. And, some put limits on the skilled nursing care that's provided, forcing Mom and Dad to pay for care.

Financial Considerations of Continuing Care Communities

Most of the residents in continuing care communities are fairly well off financially, and for good reason. Continuing care communities are expensive places to live. Entrance fees can range from $30,000 to $300,000 or more, depending on the type of dwellings offered. And, monthly fees can vary from $500 to $3,500, depending on they services Mom and Dad get. Needless to say, this is serious money, and, unless Mom and Dad are seriously loaded, will take a good chunk out of their assets. If they have sufficient savings and a house that will bring a high selling price, a continuing care community could be a good choice. They should be sure, however, that they have the resources to pay the monthly fee for as long as they might be there.

Of course, paying for continuing care is a type of insurance policy. Most continuing care communities offer several options for health care. Your parents can choose a full plan that covers all their nursing care for as long as they need it, or a plan under which they'd pay for certain aspects of care. They also can choose a fee-for-service plan, which requires them to pay for their own health needs or have insurance that pays. Before they hand over a good portion of their life savings to a continuing care community, however, there are a few things you should check out, in addition to those mentioned in the previous section.

Not all states regulate continuing care communities, and some communities have been found to be in financial trouble. Your parents should definitely find out which state agency, if any, regulates the community in which they're interested. When Mom and Dad find the regulating agency, they should inquire about the financial health of the community. They also should check whether the community is accredited by the Continuing Care Accreditation Commission (CCAC). They can do this by calling the CCAC at 202-783-2242.

Senior Apartments

Senior apartments can be built and run privately, although many are constructed and maintained by the Department of Housing and Urban Development (HUD). HUD housing is intended for low-income seniors, and is subsidized by the government. The eligibility for this type of housing varies from state to state, so you'll need to inquire with your local housing authority if you want to see if Dad qualifies.

HUD housing often is called Section 202 housing. There often is a wait for this type of housing, so if you think Dad is interested and would qualify, it's a good idea to look into it well before he's ready to move.

Because this type of housing is built exclusively for seniors and uses federal money, it must be fully handicapped accessible. Most senior apartments have dining rooms where residents may eat, although many include individual kitchens. Some community agencies offer services on site at senior apartments, and many senior apartments have their own bus or van to transport residents to the doctor, grocery store, or so forth.

Senior apartments allow Dad to have his own living space at an affordable cost. It is not assisted living, however, so he needs to be able to take care of daily chores like dressing and bathing by himself.

Privately built and run apartments for seniors are on the increase as our population ages. These vary greatly in size, price, and amenities.

Assisted Living Facilities

We hear a lot about assisted living and assisted living facilities, but many people aren't sure exactly what these terms mean. Let's start the discussion on assisted living facilities by learning exactly what assisted living is.

Assisted living is a level of care that's somewhere between independent living and nursing home care. It varies greatly because every person in an assisted living facility may have different levels of need. Those in the field of geriatrics say that people in assisted living generally need help with activities of daily living, such as dressing, bathing, eating, and using the bathroom. Assisted living also provides, or provides help with, tasks such as using a telephone, taking medicine, cooking, managing finances, using transportation, and so forth. Most provide three meals a day, with residents eating together in a dining room. Many offer transportation to doctor appointments, shopping, and other locations; activities and recreation; and housekeeping and laundry services.

If Dad is at the point where the chores and tasks of everyday life are difficult for him, assisted living might be a very good idea. Many people resist moving to an assisted living facility because they don't want to give up their independence, only to find that they really like it once they get there. Think about it. If Dad's living by himself, and having a difficult time of it, he may welcome the ease of assisted living. No more hassles with cooking and cleaning up, no more laundry, no more dusting the living room. In addition, many people welcome the opportunities for socialization that assisted living provides.

An assisted living facility can be anything from a huge, hotel-like complex (in fact, the hotel chain Marriott has entered the assisted living arena with its Brighton Gardens communities) to a large home that's been renovated to accommodate a dozen or so residents. Assisted living is most commonly provided in residential facilities, but also can be provided in adult day-care. When we talk about an assisted living facility, however, it's normally in reference to a place where Dad will live.

Something important to remember is that assisted living facilities are not nursing homes. While some facilities accept high-need residents, most do not take people who suffer from dementia or who are incontinent. If Dad needs an intensive level of care, he may not be a candidate for assisted living.

Locating an Assisted Living Facility

When you start checking out assisted living facilities, there are some important considerations to keep in mind. You're going to have to ask a lot of questions and get a lot of information before you can decide if a facility is right for Dad.

Staff members at an assisted living facility should be happy to sit down and spend as much time with you as you require. They also should be happy to show you the entire facility. If you get the feeling that the staff is trying to hide something, or if no staff person is available to meet with you, head for another place.

Assisted living facilities for the most part are regulated by government agencies such as the department of health, the department of labor and industry, and the department of agriculture. That's because they must comply with various codes in regard to fire and safety, food service, building, and so forth. Most assisted living centers are not required to meet the same standards of care that nursing homes are, and are not licensed in standard of care. That's why it's really important that you find out how an assisted living facility operates if you're considering it as a home for Dad.

If you're looking for assisted living for Mom or Dad and you don't live in the same area, you can get an idea of what's available there from Assisted Living Info, an on-line national directory of assisted living facilities. It's located on the Internet at www.assistedlivinginfo.com.

Some questions to ask and considerations to keep in mind when hunting for an assisted living facility are listed below. But, remember to trust your instincts. If you get a great feeling about a place because it's bright and clean, and the residents and staff are pleasant and smiling, that means a lot. On the other hand, if a place smells bad, the staff is rushed and unfriendly, and residents appear to be neglected, that's not a place where you want your father to be, regardless of how good its laundry service may be.

- Is there custodial care? Will Dad have help getting dressed, shaving, showering, and so forth?
- Will he have his own room or share a room? If he shares, how will he be matched with a roommate? Will he have his own bathroom?
- What services are provided for the basic monthly fee? Will he get three meals a day (check out a menu if you can)? Is laundry service included? Housekeeping? Transportation?
- What's the philosophy of the facility? Does it encourage residents to be active? Does it respect their privacy? Is it a caring place?
- What's the ratio of residents to staff members? What are the positions of staff members (nurses, aides, administrators, etc.) How many residents are there? How many spaces for residents?
- What will happen if Dad gets sick? Will the facility call a doctor to come in, or will Dad have to go out? Does Dad need to have his own doctor, or is there one associated with the facility? Is there any nursing care available? Will meals be delivered to his room if he can't get to the dining room? Will someone make sure he gets the medicine he needs? If he needs to go to the hospital, will his room be available when he returns?
- What activities are offered, and how often? Are there opportunities for outings? Are the activities varied and interesting?

You'll no doubt think of questions you want to ask in addition to these. It's a good idea to take a list of questions with you, and don't allow staff members to rush you. Assisted living is a big step for Dad, and you want to make sure he gets into the best place possible. You can check out the reputations of assisted living centers by checking with the local senior center or area agency on aging, the state department of health, the chamber of commerce, and the better business bureau.

Paying for Assisted Living

Assisted living may be great for Dad and give you real peace of mind, but somebody's going to have to pay for it.

The cost of assisted living varies tremendously, but it can run anywhere from $350 to $3,500 a month, depending on location and services offered. Medicare and most private insurances don't pay for assisted living. If Dad is low income and getting Medicaid, he may have limited coverage. Some states provide rent subsidies for assisted living, or he may be eligible for Supplemental Security Income (SSI). If Dad gets both Medicaid and SSI, he could use both those incomes to pay for assisted living. Check with your local area agency on aging to see if Dad might qualify for financial assistance.

Nursing Homes

No one likes to think about sending a parent to a nursing home, but there sometimes is just no choice. If Mom has Alzheimer's disease or anther type of dementia, is incontinent, can't move, or is just too sick for you to care for and no longer qualifies for assisted living, she may need the skilled care of a nursing home staff.

Most nursing homes provide 24-hour nursing care, on-call physicians, personal care, meals and nutritional monitoring, laundry, activities, therapy, rehabilitation services, and counseling. Patients with different needs normally are placed in different sections of the building. Alzheimer's patients, for instance, may live in a separate wing. People who are in the nursing home temporarily for rehabilitation services after a stroke or illness may be housed in a certain area.

It used to be that nursing homes were not as well regulated as they are today, and some of them were pretty bad. Truthfully, some nursing homes still aren't great, but there are a lot more people involved these days with monitoring them, and a lot more rules and regulations with which nursing homes must comply. All nursing homes have to be licensed, and they're inspected by state and federal agencies.

Most nursing homes today provide good care to their patients. While nursing homes were often thought of as "a place where you go to die," today they are places where elderly people go to get the care they need, make new friends, and participate in a variety of activities. My grandmother entered a county-run nursing home in Pennsylvania when she was 101 years old. The staff there immediately got her involved in the craft room, where she still, at almost 103, spends some of her mornings drinking coffee and painting salt and pepper shakers, plates, and pitchers.

Dealing with Tough Decisions

Acknowledging the fact that your mother needs to be in a nursing home won't be easy. Hopefully, she'll agree that she needs the level of care a nursing home provides, and she'll accept the move.

Even if she doesn't complain about going, you'll probably experience guilt and sadness about the move. If she resists the idea and is bitter and angry at you for encouraging the move, the situation may seem impossible. It becomes even more agonizing if other family members disagree with your decision that mom needs nursing home care.

To be frank, families have broken apart over the nursing home issue. Your brother can't understand why Mom can't continue to be on her own. So what if she forgets to turn the stove off now and then? Or, why can't she live with you? You have room in your house, don't you? These arguments are extremely emotional and can be tremendously draining, It's perfectly understandable that you might be tempted to give in and agree with your brother.

If you are Mom's primary caregiver, however, and you know in your heart and your mind that she needs to be in a nursing home, then you've got to stand firm in your decision. If you simply can't take care of her, she can't take care of herself, and she's past the point of an assisted living facility, a nursing home is the answer.

Paying for a Nursing Home

Once you decide that Mom needs to be in a nursing home, the next step is to figure out how to pay for her care. According to the American Association of Retired Persons, the average cost of a nursing home is nearly $50,000 a year. The other bad news is that Medicare doesn't cover the cost, except sometimes for a short period if a patient is admitted to a nursing home after a stay in the hospital. All in all, Medicare pays less than 10 percent of all nursing home bills.

If Mom is in a nursing home after a hospital stay and qualifies for Medicare funding, be sure to check her Medigap policy. Some Medigap plans pay some nursing home expenses that Medicare doesn't cover.

So, who pays? About 30 percent of all nursing home residents pay the costs themselves. A few have long-term health insurance that pays for them. And, nearly 70 percent receive assistance from Medicaid, the state-administered aid program. Many people living in nursing homes and receiving Medicaid started out paying for their care on their own. As you can image, however, at $50,000 a year, a savings account is quickly depleted. When a person's assets are down to a certain level, Medicaid kicks in.

Most nursing homes reserve a certain number of beds for Medicare and Medicaid patients. The bad thing is, if Mom starts off paying her own tab, then goes on Medicaid when her savings are nearly gone, the nursing home doesn't have to give her one of those beds. When you're looking for a nursing home, be sure to find out the exact policy of each home regarding this situation. You don't want Mom to have to move to another nursing home, or, worse yet, be left without a home.

If your parent is a veteran, he or she might qualify for funding for nursing home care from the Department of Veterans Affairs. Call your local veterans affairs office to find out if there's money available for your parent.

And, many nursing homes are affiliated with a particular church or religious group that helps to support the home financially. If Mom is at one of these homes, there may be some money available through the church for residents who need help paying their monthly bill. You and other family members should get together before Mom enters a nursing home to examine the options and decide how you'll pay for it.

Finding the Best Home You Can

Naturally, you want Mom to be in a nice, pleasant facility, and for her to receive the best possible care. But, how do you go about finding that place?

If you live in an area where there aren't a lot of nursing homes, your choices will be limited. If you're in or around a city, however, you're likely to have a lot of homes from which to choose. To make your search easier, you can start by checking the latest inspection reports on the nursing homes in which you're interested. These reports can be found on Medicare's web site, which is at www.medicare.gov. You just enter the name of the home to get the inspection results. You also can search by county so you can compare all the nursing homes in one area.

Once you've checked the inspection reports, start asking around. Just as when you're looking for a good doctor, a good restaurant, or a nice hotel, you can get idea of what's available by asking around. If you have friends whose parents are in nursing homes, where are they? What do your friends think of the homes? Are their parents happy there? What services are offered? Are their parents well cared for? How expensive is it?

After you've narrowed your search to a few places, be sure to call each one and find out if there's space available. Mom may have to be put on a waiting list.

Of course, you don't want to rely solely on the opinions of a few people, but knowing their experiences and feelings about a particular nursing home is a good place to start. You'll need to meet with representatives of the nursing homes in which you're interested. This is the time to ask all your questions about care and services, cost, payment options, and so forth. Find out if the home, the administrator, and staff all are certified, and make sure all staff members must have background checks before they can be hired. Many of the questions you'll need to ask will be the same as those recommended when looking for an assisted living facility. Refer back to that list for some ideas. And, don't forget to write down your questions before you meet with the nursing home representative.

You'll also need to visit the nursing homes that you're considering. This is the only way you'll get a good feeling for how the home is run and the condition of it and its residents. Some things to look for are listed below.

- **Cleanliness.** Does the home look and smell clean?
- **Atmosphere.** Is the atmosphere cheerful or gloomy? Is it light and sunny, or dark? How's the temperature? Are there visitors there and activities going on? Does the facility attempt to make patients' rooms homey by allowing them to bring personal items and hang photos on the walls?
- **Residents.** Do the residents look clean and well groomed? Do they seem to be enjoying themselves? Do they socialize with one another?
- **Staff.** Does the staff spend much time interacting with residents? Are staff members friendly and helpful? Do they seem rushed or overworked? Do they complain to residents and family members about the home? Do they respond quickly to residents' needs? Is there enough staff at nights and on holidays?

- **Dining facilities.** Try to visit the dining room during mealtime. Do residents seem to be enjoying their meals? Are they rushed through, or allowed to take their time? Are there aides available to help residents who need help and to monitor food intake? Do residents have choices regarding their food?
- **Safety.** Are there handrails in the hallways? Are exits clearly marked? Are measures taken to make sure residents can't leave the facility without someone knowing of their whereabouts? Must visitors sign in? Is there limited access to the facility? Are there adequate smoke detectors and sprinklers? Are the hallways kept clear?

A great resource to keep in mind in is the local ombudsman. The area agency on aging runs the federal Long-Term Care Ombudsman program, which is assigned to every nursing home in your community. The ombudsman appointed by the program is a person who helps resolve conflicts between nursing homes and patients, or families of patients. He also reports suspected neglect or abuse. Every nursing home is required to post the name and phone number of the ombudsman who is assigned there. If you have questions about a nursing home, or complaints or concerns once Mom is there, the ombudsman is the person to call.

Once Mom is Settled In

Once Mom has gotten settled into a nursing home, you can help to make the experience of living there as pleasant as possible. If she's able, you can take her out now and then to give her a change of scenery and keep life interesting.

If she enjoys company, encourage other family members and friends to visit. Try to coordinate the visits so she has people with her frequently, but tell visitors to be aware of signs that Mom might be getting tired. Help her make her room as homelike as possible with photos of family and friends, and mementos from her own home.

If Mom shares a room, get to know her roommate and visit with her a bit when you arrive or before you leave. Get to know as many of the staff as you can, too, and feel free to ask questions about Mom's care, or express any concerns you might have.

Pay close attention to how Mom appears. Is she well groomed and clean? Does she seem to be maintaining her weight? Is she enjoying the food? What's her schedule like? Is she busy enough? Is she getting enough sleep?

Nursing homes are places of care, and hopefully, of caring. You can be Mom's advocate while she's there, working along with the staff to make her stay as pleasant and satisfying as possible. Speak up for her, and keep a close watch on her care and her health. Remember that she's the customer, and the staff of a nursing home is there to care for her and serve her.

Regardless of what housing option you and your parents choose, your parents will be happiest when their voices are heard and their wishes taken into consideration. Include them in discussions whenever possible, and listen to their concerns and opinions. Regardless of whether they live with you, in their own home, in a shared-housing situation, assisted living, a retirement community, or a nursing home, they should be treated with respect and dignity. They are, after all, your parents.

Chapter 8

Taking Care of Yourself

A few years ago, a good friend was juggling the responsibilities of a full-time job, her own family, and helping to care for her mother, who was dying of cancer. Every day she would go to work, leave her office in northern New Jersey at 5 p.m., and drive 40 minutes to her parent's home, or later, into New York City, where her mother was hospitalized. After keeping vigil at her mother's bedside for several hours, she'd drive home to see her son before he went to bed, visit with her husband, look at the day's mail, throw in a load of laundry, and prepare for the next day.

While talking one night, I asked my friend why she insisted on keeping up this routine for so many weeks, at such physical and emotional expense to herself and her own family.

She said, "It's how I was raised. It's what I do."

I never forgot her answer, and came to understand her words exactly when my own father became very ill a couple of years later. We care for our aging parents because they cared for us. They showed us how to care, and now, it's just what we do—or will someday do. We care, because it's our turn to.

If we're not actively caring for aging parents at this time, we all probably know plenty of people who are. I talk with friends almost every day who are caring for—and worrying about—parents and in-laws. One's concerned about her mother-in-law, who insists on carrying laundry baskets down the steep basement steps of her old home. Another worries about his father driving at night because his dad has admitted he has trouble seeing properly. One is struggling to hold his own life together as he helps a parent through the end of hers. Another drives four hours every weekend to spend time with a mother who's adjusting to assisted living. A couple wonders where they'll get the money to help keep a parent in much-needed assisted living.

"We're just at that age," we say. Care giving, however, is not restricted to those of us in our 40s, 50, and 60s. My mother, at age 77, is still caring for her 103-year-old mother.

Unfortunately, most people are almost completely unprepared to be care-givers. We step in without any training or preparation to do a job that needs to be done. And, most of us underestimate the amount of energy and emotional investment required in order to be a caregiver.

Care Giving is Hard Work

There's just no question that care giving is hard work. You may encounter more physical work than normal if you're doing your parent's laundry, helping with yard work, or even lifting an infirmed parent out of bed or his favorite chair.

Maybe your work is primarily in terms of helping with financial, business, and medical matters, so you spend a lot of time sorting through checkbooks, insurance forms, and other documents.

It's the emotional work that comes with care giving, though, that may be the most difficult. Most caregivers find themselves on an emotional roller coaster that can go on and on and on. There are good days and bad days—highs and lows, and you've got to be ready to deal with all of them.

Fortunately, the recognition given to caregivers is increasing, and, as more and more of us are called to take our turn, additional sources of help are likely to become available.

Preparing for Care giving

Most caregivers, statistics show, are women between 40 and 60 years old, who have a job, a husband, and sometimes children at home. These caregivers, as you can imagine, or perhaps know first hand, wear a lot of hats. Wife, daughter, mother, employee, homemaker.

If there is opportunity before you begin taking care of your aging parent, address each of these areas of your life, and take a good, hard look at how you, and those around you, might be affected by your care giving duties.

Your Family

Hopefully, your spouse and children will be supportive of your care giving efforts. Be prepared, however, for the possibility of friction. No one likes to feel neglected, and care giving can really cut into your time and your normal routine..

Many caregivers say that the hardest part of the job is dealing with the demands of so many people, and trying to keep everyone happy. If you're spending a lot of time with a sick parent, while at the same time trying to keep up with your workload, your social and community obligations, and your son's baseball schedule, you're likely to be headed for a big-time case of burnout.

If you have children still living at home, you should explain to them what you'll be doing in the way of care giving, and how those duties may impact on your time with them. Perhaps you'll need to miss a swim meet or basketball game now and then, or won't be able to be a band parent this year. If you can, get your kids involved in a limited way in helping with the caregiving situation. Older children might drive a grandparent to a doctor's appointment or pick up medicine at the pharmacy. Even younger children can sit and read a story to a sick grandparent, or simply talk about what's going on at school.

If a parent is coming to live at your house, it's more important than ever to sit down with all family members and discuss how the situation will impact on each person. Does somebody have to give up a bedroom in order to make room for Grandmom? Will you and your husband be able to maintain privacy? Will the kids feel comfortable having their friends over?

Think carefully about how caring for an elderly parent may affect your own family. Care giving is a loving, generous act, but it shouldn't come at the expense of your relationship with your spouse and kids. If you're afraid that caring for an aging or ill parent will cause too much strain on your family life, you'll need to plan for a good support system from which you can get all the help you'll need.

Your Employer

If you're plunged into a care giving situation without warning, as is often the case, you'll have little opportunity to plan how you'll balance your new responsibilities with those of your job. If you have some lead time, however, it's a good idea to think about how you'll handle this balancing act, and then discuss your tactics with your employer.

Many people have tried to keep up with work while also performing care giving duties, only to find themselves in over their heads and out of favor with their bosses. You know the reason you didn't finish that important report was because you had to get Mom to her doctor's appointment over your lunch hour. Or, you know that you've been late three times this week because you had to drop off Dad at adult day care. Without knowing your situation, however, you boss—and you co-workers—may just assume you're not interested in doing your job.

As you did with your family situation, take a good, hard look at how you'll manage work and care giving. If it seems to be an impossible deal, you might have to ask for some time off, or work out another arrangement with your employer. Some suggestions for dealing with the work/care giving situation are listed below.

- Be up front with your employer about your situation, but don't feel that you have to ask his permission to care for your parent. He's entitled to know about a life situation that may affect your ability to do your job effectively, but whether or not to commit to caring for a parent is your decision. Many employers are willing—even happy—to work with employees to assure that the situation remains satisfactory for everyone.
- Check your company's policy on care giving issues. Is there an employee assistance program? Many companies offer benefits or provide services that could help you. It's in the best interest of the company, after all, to ensure that employees are able to be effective at work while handling non-work situations.
- Look into the Family and Medical Leave Act. Passed by Congress in 1993, the act mandates all public agencies (including public schools) and employers with 50 or more employees to give at least 12 weeks of unpaid leave to any worker who is caring for a family member who is seriously ill. A family member is defined as a spouse, child, or parent. The employee must have worked for the company for at least 12 months, and have worked for at least 1,250 hours during the past 12 months. Your employer doesn't have to give you the same position when you return, but it has to be a comparable one with equivalent duties, salary, and benefits.
- Inquire as to whether your schedule could be changed. If your sister can care for Dad until 3 p.m., perhaps your employer would be willing to let

you work from 6:30 a.m. until 2:30 p.m. so you could take over for Sis when she leaves. Maybe you could get a day off during the week and work on Saturday. Many employers are finding the need to be flexible with schedules in order to keep employees happy and productive. This may be especially feasible in a smaller company.

- Be creative. Come up with a plan for job sharing, working from home, stretching out vacation days to give you long weekends, or some other innovative solution to your problem. Present the plan to your boss in a positive way, explaining how it will allow you to continue being effective at your job, while accommodating your other obligations.

- Don't mix care giving and your job. Keep the two obligations as separate as possible. Don't for instance, spend the morning on your office telephone trying to locate an adult day-care facility for Dad. On the other hand, don't neglect to give Dad the attention he needs at home while you attempt to finish up your report for work.

- Check out how others in similar circumstances have coped with balancing care giving with work and family. The American Association of Retired Persons web site offers a discussion board for caregivers. You can find it on the Internet at www.aarp.org/indexes/health.html#caregiving. The Family Caregiver Alliance also provides discussion groups and a lot of information for caregivers on its site at www.caregiver.org.

Getting Help When You Need It

We all need somebody to lean on—especially when caring for elderly parents. Because care giving can be so demanding and emotionally draining, you've got to know where to find help when it becomes necessary.

As care giving becomes a better recognized and talked-about topic, more sources of help are springing up. Some people, however, are reluctant to ask for help in any matter, taking care of elderly parents included. As a society, we tend to take pride in being able to do it all. We think we should be able to handle everything, without looking for help. Many people get up before it's light to have a cup of coffee and a quick look at the newspaper before starting a day that involves working, driving, cleaning, cooking, talking, listening, and planning for the next day.

Add care giving to that list of chores, and life can seem pretty impossible.

If you're caring for an aging parent, or think that you soon will be, do yourself a big favor, and find out now what resources are available in your area.

Support Groups

Some people tend to be distrustful or disdainful of support groups, but it often helps to talk and listen to people who have similar problems and are coping with like situations.

Children of Aging Parents (CAPS) is a non-profit organization that started in 1977 in Pennsylvania when a group of neighbors who were caring for aging parents started meeting informally to discuss their concerns and problems. The need for such a group soon became very clear, and CAPS incorporated in 1980. In 1986, advice guru Ann Landers mentioned CAPS in a newspaper column, spurring thousands of people to contact the organization.

Children of Aging Parents (CAPS) provides information and referrals for caregivers, distributes, educational materials, sponsors research regarding care giving, and maintains a speaker's bureau. It also has a website filled with information for caregivers. You can call CAPS at 800-227-7294, or find it on the Internet at www.caps4caregivers.org.

Research CAPS has sponsored shows that caregivers who participate in support groups suffer less from stress and remain healthier than those who do not. The organization refers caregivers to CAPS-affiliated support groups, and provides start-up training and support. CAPS support groups are held across the country in churches and synagogues, schools, libraries, and private homes.

There are many other support groups that deal with care giving issues, as well. Your area office on aging will be able to refer you to those in your community.

Community Services

Most communities offer a variety of services aimed at elderly residents and their families. And yet, many people aren't aware of the services available, so they fail to take advantage of them.

A great place to start is with your local area agency on aging. The Area Agency on Aging is a nationwide program that gets federal, state, and local funds, and operates in every county in the country. Local branches typically offers community workshops and seminars on topics such as care giving and long-term care insurance. Representatives of local agencies lobby for the rights and benefits of senior citizens, and provide training to the business community for better serving the elderly.

Local offices offer a variety of information on many topics relating to seniors, and specialist are available to answer questions and make referrals either in person or over the telephone. The agency also provides community-based programs and services such as specialized transportation, legal services, employment counseling for older adults, and health information and screening programs. It also typically oversees the operations of local senior centers.

Area agencies on aging in some states get funding from state lotteries, which allows them to offer services at reduced prices—or for free. If there is a fee for a service, it's likely to be on a sliding scale, based on a person's ability to pay.

The Area Agency on Aging also runs the federal Long-terms Care Ombudsman Program that's assigned to every nursing home in the community. The ombudsman handles complaints and concerns of family members and can provide information about different nursing homes to the families of prospective residents. And, local Meals on Wheels programs often are administered by area agencies on aging.

Your local area agency on aging is a great resource that you shouldn't overlook. Trying to get a handle on the resources in your community can be a daunting and time-consuming job. You can save a lot of time and trouble by contacting your local agency.

If your parent enjoys being active and with other people, check out the senior centers in your area. Remember that every center will be different, with some offering much more than others. Some services and programs you may find at a senior center include those listed below.

- Exercise classes
- Computer classes and Internet access
- Recreational events
- Trips
- Health screenings
- Programs on various topics of interest
- Transportation services
- Consumer information
- Volunteer opportunities
- Adult day care
- Free or reduced-price meals

Many older people greatly enjoy spending time at senior centers. Your parent may make some new friends, and find people with similar interests. She may end up taking a watercolor class, or learning to use a computer. If you think she may enjoy a senior center, encourage her to try it out. Offer to drive her to the center and go in with her the first time or two until she gets familiar with the situation.

If you take a look at the blue pages of your phone book, you'll probably see an impressive list of government agencies that serve elderly residents. There are health agencies, the Social Security office, a local county board of assistance, housing authorities, local offices of the American Association of Retired Persons, senior citizen councils, an Alzheimer's Association, and many more.

Congress recently reauthorized the Older Americans Act, which, among other things, creates a National Family Caregiver Support Program funded by both federal and state dollars. The program provides information and training for caregivers, assistance to caregivers in gaining access to services, respite care for caregivers, and some supplemental services. For more information on the act, see the U.S. Administration on Aging web site at www.aoa.dhhs.gov.

Don't be hesitant to contact these agencies if you think they may be useful to you and your parent. If you're not sure about which agency to call, check with your local area agency on aging for a referral.

Siblings or Other Relatives

If you're caring for an elderly parent, it's very important on several levels to involve other family members. On a practical note, you'll need the help. Even if you think now that you can care for your parent by yourself, you'll find out over time that it's nearly impossible for one person to do it all.

Two, if you don't include other family members in helping for Mom or Dad, you risk hurting their feelings, or becoming angry yourself because you'll feel that you're doing more than your share.

In most families, there's one person who takes on the role of primary caregiver. This can occur because he's the only child who lives close by the aging parent or parents. Or, perhaps he's naturally the kind of person who steps up to the plate when there's a job to be done. Maybe he has a very close relationship with Dad, and caring for him just seems like a natural thing to do.

The danger of the one-person caregiver scenario is that it can breed resentment—both on the part of the caregiver, and of other family members. If you're the primary caregiver, you may well feel that other family members aren't doing their share, and that you're carrying more than your share of the load. Family members, on the other hand, may feel shut out, and somewhat envious of the time and relationship you have with the parent. Feelings stemming from old sibling rivalries can come back after many years of having been put aside. Tempers flare, and words are spoken that everyone later regrets.

Involving all siblings in your parents' care—and other family member, if you wish—is a smart idea. And, it can considerably ease your burden.

Make a list of all chores that need to be done, and assign some jobs to each involved member of the family. Even siblings who live far away can help with jobs such as writing checks and researching topics of concern. Make sure that each person understands exactly what he's responsible for. It may be a good idea to rotate chores, so that they're evenly divided. Some of the chores you can assign to various family members are listed below.

- Grocery shopping. Everyone needs to shop for groceries, so ask one family member to pick up the items Mom needs and deliver them to her home. Don't forget that Mom may need help getting the groceries put away.
- Running errands. Keep a list of errands, and ask the family member for whom it's most convenient to do them. If your sister lives only a block from the library, for instance, it wouldn't be difficult for her to return Dad's book and pick up another one for him. If you drive by the drugstore on your way to work every day, you're the logical choice for picking up Mom's medicine.
- Cooking meals. If your sister cooks for her family every night, ask her to make a little more. She can either deliver the food to your parents immediately, or put individual portions in the freezer for them to use later.
- Visiting. Work out a schedule to ensure that Mom has frequent visitors, without the same person having to go every time. Enlist all applicable family members—grandkids make great visitors.
- Helping with yard work. If you're not hiring someone to cut grass and trim hedges, ask a family member to help out.
- Doing laundry. We all know how fast laundry piles up. Enlist a family member to handle washing and drying Mom's clothing, sheets, towels, and so forth.

- Giving you a break. If you're spending every evening with Dad so you can make sure he eats dinner, takes his medicine, and gets safely into bed, don't hesitate to ask a sibling or other family member to take a turn once or twice a week.
- If family members aren't willing to help with care giving for an elderly parent, ask them to contribute financially so you can pay for help. You also can lighten your burden by asking family members to pick up a bigger share of the work at your house. If you're spending six hours a day at your parent's home, chances are some chores at your own place have gone to the back burner or beyond.

Remember that you may be able to handle the extra work of care giving by yourself for a while, but you'll eventually pay a high price.

Paying for Help

You may have to consider paying for outside services. The good news is that there is help available. The bad news is that paying for that help can get to be an expensive venture. Still, one person can only do so much, and some tasks may be next to impossible for you. There are different types and levels of help available, all of which fall into the broad category of home health care.

If Mom needs help with everyday chores such as cooking meals, doing laundry, cleaning the house, or keeping track of her medicine, she needs homemaker, or companion care. If she requires assistance with bathing, using the toilet, feeding herself, dressing, taking medicine, or getting in and out of bed, she needs a home health care aide.

If she requires even more extensive care, you'll need to find someone qualified to provide skilled nursing care. Probably the easiest and safest way to find someone to provide home health care is to work through a home health care agency. Most of these are able to provide all levels of care, and many of them are bonded. Be sure to find out if the agency is certified by a state or federal agency. If it receives reimbursements from Medicare or Medicaid, it is required by law to meet certain safety and care standards, and employees must undergo certain training programs.

You also could contact your local area agency on aging for recommendations and referrals for home health care workers. And, someone at the agency may be able to tell you of any of your home health care costs would be covered by your parent's insurance. Care ordered by Mom or Dad's doctor usually will be covered by Medicare, Medicaid, or a Medi-gap policy. Services such as laundry, cooking, and cleaning, however, probably will not be.

If there's no family member or friend available to cut Dad's lawn, trim hedges or wash windows, consider hiring a service or a teenager in the neighborhood.

Adult Day Care

If your parent isn't capable of being on his own all day, there's no family member or friend who can stay with him, and you prefer not to hire home health care, you may want to consider adult day care.

These usually are all-day programs, although you may be able to take Dad for only part of the day, if you wish. Normally, Dad can go as many days a week as you want him to. Adult day care facilities are supervised, and should offer a variety of programs and activities to keep him alert and interested.

Some adult day cares offer counseling and support programs for family members, and many can provide speech therapy, memory therapy, reality orientation, or exercise classes to their clients.

If you're considering adult day care, be sure to visit the ones in your area and see how they compare. Ask how many staff member each one has, and how many clients. There should be one staff member for every five or six clients. If Dad is resistant to the idea, stay with him for a while for the first day or two until he gets used to the surroundings and the other clients.

When It Might Be Necessary to Quit Care Giving

You've been having trouble sleeping for the past three or four months. You wake up in the middle of the night and lie awake for a long time, thinking about what you need to do, what you should have done, or what you wish you hadn't done.

You and your spouse barely talk to each other any more, much less enjoy good times together the way you used to. You haven't been out together for months, and your love life has stopped completely.

You've lost 15 pounds over the past few months, and when you eat, it's only because you know you have to. You have no interest in buying food, cooking, or eating.

Your best friend has left phone messages for you three times in the past week, but you don't bother to call her back to talk. You start checking your caller ID before you pick up the phone because you just don't feel like talking to anyone.

Your adult children are telling you that they're worried about you, and they're upset because you've spent hardly any time with the grandkids lately. You don't want to tell them that the grandkids seem too noisy and boisterous for you right now.

You've stopped taking a shower and washing your hair every day because it seems like too much trouble. You're always tired and you know you look awful, but it just doesn't seem to matter.

Your employer has told you that your level of work has dropped dramatically, and that if the situation doesn't improve, you could be looking at a demotion. The news upsets you, but you can't think of any way to make things better.

You were never a big drinker, but you've started having two or three—sometimes more—drinks every night before you go to bed. You tell your family members that the drinks help you to sleep better.

You're irritable, upset, and often cry for no apparent reason. You feel on edge, pulled in all directions, and unable to focus or concentrate. You know you're not happy, but you can't pinpoint the reason. You feel anxious, moody, and nervous.

If one or two of these scenarios hits home with you, you should be warned that the stress and responsibilities of care giving just might be starting to take their toll. If three, four, or more of the scenarios sound familiar, it's time to give serious thought to throwing in the towel. These situations can eventually lead to anxiousness, resentment, and depression.

If you even think there's a chance that you may be suffering from depression, or others have suggested the possibility to you, you should see your doctor immediately. Explain to him what you've been doing, and tell him how you're feeling. Depression can be treated, but not until it's been diagnosed.

If you feel extremely angry or resentful toward your parent, or have been tempted to physically harm her, you need to remove yourself from the care giving situation. If this is the case, don't blame yourself, or feel that you've failed. If you need to quit taking care of Mom, assure yourself that you did the best you could for as long as you could. Get others to help decide the next step for Mom's care. Now may be the time to get her into a good nursing home or assisted care facility.

Consult other family members, your doctor, or a counselor. You must not risk jeopardizing your own health in order to continue caring for an elderly parent. Your parent wouldn't want that for you, nor do the other people who love you. It's time to do what's best for everyone—including you.

Chapter 9

Dealing With Death and Dying

One of the most difficult of all life experiences is dealing with the death of someone you love—a parent, spouse, friend, or child. If death occurs in its natural progression, you'll lose your parents before your spouse, contemporaries and children. Many of us already have lost a mother or father, and are trying to help the other one as he or she moves along with life. Some of us are anticipating the death of a parent who has been diagnosed with a terminal illness. Some of us will be shocked some morning soon when we get a call that a parent has died suddenly, or when we discover the body of a parent who has died.

No matter how many times you experience death, or how prepared you think you are for the death of a loved one, it still is shocking and often devastating when it occurs. Many people who have cared for parents through the final days of life say that when the expected death finally occurs, they find themselves totally unprepared to deal with it.

Hopefully, you and your parents have discussed their philosophies concerning health care, and you know their wishes concerning topics like resuscitation, life support and so forth. Having a clear understanding of those wishes makes dealing with medical decisions a lot easier, and also gives your parents some control over what will happen to them. Talking with your parents about what kind of funeral they would like to have also is a good idea. Pre-planning and pre-paying for a funeral may make financial sense, as well.

Nobody likes to talk about death—whether it's his own, or the death of loved one. Since we all some day will die, however, not talking about it is simply a means of avoiding something that's inevitable. Whether your parent dies unexpectedly, or after a long illness, you'll get a lot of reassurance from having known ahead of time about his wishes concerning a funeral, burial, and so forth.

Helping a Parent Deal With End-of-Life Issues

If your parent discovers that she's terminally ill, she'll need all the help and support you can offer. A serious illness has the capacity to turn lives upside down. It launches both the person who is sick and her caregivers onto an emotional roller coaster, while at the same time issuing practical challenges regarding such things such as nursing care and medical bills.

Learning that your mother or father is dying sets off a series of reactions and emotions within you that you'll need to work through. You may feel angry or unable to accept that your parent soon will die. You might wonder how you'll get along without the parent on whom you've depended for so many things. You may have unresolved issues you're your parent that you need to resolve.

While you're dealing with your own emotions, you're also going to have to help Mom to cope with hers, and with the physical aspects of her illness. Terminal illness is extremely challenging, both for the person who is sick, and for those who love and care for her. It also, however, can be a time of bonding and loving. Caring for a parent at the end of his or her life will be one of the most difficult tasks you ever undertake. It also can be one of the most rewarding.

Most people don't talk about end-of-life issues until they're directly faced with the prospect of dying. Even then, many people try to avoid the subject. The best time to discuss end-of-life issues is before Mom or Dad gets sick. End-of-life issues are part of life, and much easier to discuss before the end of life is in sight. There are legal and financial considerations to dying, as well as spiritual and emotional ones. You can help your parent to resolve these issues by talking about what he wants to happen at the time of his death.

My aunt and uncle died during the past year within eight months of each other. Each death was sudden. My uncle knew exactly what his wife wished to have happen when she died, and she had a living will that her family used as a guide when she suddenly became very ill. My cousins, in turn, knew exactly what their father's wishes were for his funeral and burial. Not having to wonder if they were doing the right thing, or guess at their dad's wishes made the trauma of having both their parents die within such a short time a little easier for them.

Talking About It

As a society, we're pretty mum about the topic of death. We take great pains to avoid thinking or talking about it. We use phrases such as, "if anything should ever happen to me," instead of, "if I should die unexpectedly." We avoid even saying the words "died" or "dead," couching them instead with phrases such as "passed away," and "at rest."

The fact is, however, if your mom has just learned that she has cancer and only three or four months to live, chances are, unless she's in denial, that she's going to want to talk about it. Her impending death is the most important issue facing her, and she'll need someone to help her deal with it. Being willing to hear her out and to let her freely discuss her fears and frustrations can help to put her mind at ease and bring comfort to her.

She might want to contact friends or relatives with whom she's been out of touch. She may want to visit, or have visitors. She might want to write letters or keep a journal. Maybe she wants to plan her funeral, update her will, or make sure her medical directives are in order. Unless you're willing to talk about these sorts of things with her, however, she may feel reluctant to tell you what she wants.

It's vitally important to try to overcome your own discomfort concerning death and death-related issues in order to give your parent the chance to deal with her death on her own terms. Granted, it's not easy to talk to someone you love about the fact that she soon will die. Many people find they simply can't do it. If you're able to get past your own discomfort, though, you'll be offering a precious gift of compassion and love.

Not everyone who is dying, of course, will want to talk about the illness and death. Some people prefer to keep on living as normally as possible for as long as they can, almost as if they aren't sick at all. Some terminally ill patients actively deny their illness and the fact that they soon will die.

Accepting death does not mean that the person who is dying gives up all hope. There have been cases in which cancer suddenly and inexplicably goes into remission, or a tumor disappears. Accepting death means finding peace with the fact that it will—either soon or later—occur.

Take your cue from your parent. If she doesn't want to talk about her illness or death, don't force her to. If she does want to talk, however, be there for her as much as you're able. Even if you don't know what to say, being willing to listen to her fears and concerns will be a comfort to her.

Accepting an Impending Death

Our society's attention turned to death in 1969, when a doctor named Elisabeth Kubler-Ross wrote a book that, among other things, identified five stages that dying person often progresses through. Those stages, according to Kubler-Ross, are:

- Denial and isolation. When learning that they have a terminal disease, most people will deny it. They tell themselves the doctor is wrong, the diagnosis is a mistake, the doctor must have confused them with some other patient. This stage can be unsettling for family members to deal with, but is a normal part of the process. It gives the dying person time to absorb the shock and to prepare himself for dealing with dying. In rare instances, a person will deny the approaching death vehemently, even to the point of planning a long trip for the future or buying a new home.

- Anger or resentment. Once the dying person has stopped denying the approaching death, she often reacts with anger. "Why me?" is a common question during this stage of anger, which may be directed toward medical personnel, family members, God, or whoever. If your parent seems angry at you during this stage, try not to take it personally. It's extremely difficult to take, but if you've been a caregiver to your mom, some of her anger may be directed toward you. You may be tempted to return her anger, but don't. It only will fuel her resentment and make the situation worse. Plus, you're likely to regret it later.

- Bargaining. During this stage, a dying person will bargain with God, or with fate, or whatever. He may try to bargain for more time, saying something like, "listen God, if you just let me live another year so that I can see my grandson graduate from college, I won't ask for any more time." Kubler-Ross compares this tactic to a child who has been told she can't sleep over at her friend's house. She may stomp her feet and throw a tantrum, much like the dying person did during the anger stage. Then, she tries to bargain for the privilege of sleeping at her friend's house, offering to do extra chores and be on her very best behavior. A dying person may offer to devote his life to the church if God allows him to live. Some patients have volunteered to donate their bodies to science once they finally die if doctors use that scientific knowledge to extend their lives. Some people take a more active interest in their health care during this stage, perhaps looking for cures or alternative treatments. If this occurs with Dad, be supportive and take time to listen to his hopes and concerns.

- Depression. This stage occurs when the dying person can no longer pretend that he's going to get better, or deny his illness. Maybe he's found out that the last operation didn't accomplish what everyone had hoped it would and he'll need another operation. Or, maybe he's terribly worried and depressed about how his illness will affect his family's financial health. Another cause of depression is that the dying person is beginning to grieve for the loss of his live and all that he loves. Family members can be reassuring concerning practical matters like finances. You can reassure Dad that his insurance covered the cost of the operation and that there's been no need to touch his savings account. Don't, however, try to talk him out of his depression that stems from the realization that his life will soon be over.

- Acceptance. When the patient has stopped denying that she's going to die, the anger and bargaining have ended, and the depression has subsided (at least somewhat) she may reach a stage of acceptance concerning her impending death. Generally, when this happens, she'll become quiet, withdrawn, and desire more time alone. She may avoid conversation, and probably will have little interest in what's going on around her. This is not the time for cheery conversation and gossip. Perhaps she'll like to have quiet, soothing music playing, or to have a family member simply sit alongside of her. Don't feel as though you have to fill up the silence—it will be comforting to Mom to just know you're with her. If she wants to talk, however, by all means be willing to listen.

Not every person goes through each of these stages in the order that they're listed. And, it's important to know that these stages don't occur in a neat, predictable fashion. Your mother might seem accepting of her approaching death one day, and then angry and resentful the next. The stages may overlap, or Mom may seem to pass through a particular stage and then regress. And, some people skip stages entirely. Not everyone reaches the stage of acceptance.

Recognizing these stages that your parent may pass through may make the process of her dying more real to you, and help you to accept the fact that she won't be with you much longer.

Caring for a Parent at the End of Life

The period during which your parent is very sick or dying will be extremely emotional and draining. You'll dread hearing the phone ring, thinking each time it does that it's going to bring bad news. You may dread going to visit Dad because you don't know what to say to him, or it makes you feel awful to see him so sick.

If Mom is dying in her home, with Dad as her primary caregiver, you may find yourself getting very angry with your father for asking you for help so often. You may resent your brother or sister who lives far away and isn't dealing with the day-to-day anguish of watching a parent at the end of life. If that's the case, incidentally, you should remember that your brother might be suffering through Mom's illness just as intensely as you are, despite the fact that he's halfway across the country. He may feel extremely guilty that he's not able to be around, and isolated in his sorrow.

You might feel angry at hospital personnel for not being able to do more for your father, or angry at yourself because he's in a hospital instead of in your home.

As Dad becomes sicker and sicker, you may be tempted to visit less and less. You don't know what to say, and it's uncomfortable to be around. Although it may be easier now to make up excuses not to go, be aware that you're likely to regret it later. You don't need to be bubbly and chatty when you visit. Just sitting with Dad is enough.

While trying to deal with all these emotions, you'll also need to be dealing with some practical matters. Who's going to take care of Mom? Will she remain in her home with nursing care when it becomes necessary? Is there enough money to be able to do that? How much will her insurance cover? Can Mom move in with you? If so, what sort of changes must be made to your house in order to accommodate her? If she moves in with a sibling, how should you divide the responsibility for care giving? Should she go to the hospital? If so, when? Would you consider hospice care? Would she?

Hopefully, you'll be able to sit down with Mom and talk about these and any other applicable matters. If she's learned that she has a terminal illness but is still feeling fairly well, you might be able to resolve a lot of these kinds of questions and let her have as much control over the situation as possible.

As a society of caregivers, many of us seem to be moving in a circle back to the time when nearly all elderly, sick, and dying persons were cared for by their families—at home. Family members cleared out a space for Grandmother's bed, and cared for her until she died. Then came the hospital movement, where we shied away from the unpleasantness and messiness often associated with sickness and death by sending our loved ones off to spend their last days in an institution. Now, we seem anxious to explore our options. Even if we can't care for Mom in our home, we may not have to let her die alone in a hospital. We're realizing, both as patients and caregivers, that we have options, and that death doesn't have to be cold and impersonal and lonely. Let's explore some of the options available for people and families of people who are nearing the end life.

How Much Can You Do?

How you'll help to care for your parent in the last weeks or months of her life depends on many factors. What you need to determine before you make any plans at all, is how much you're realistically able to do. To get that answer, you'll have to consider emotional, practical, and financial aspects of care giving. You'll need to look at how much time you have. Most of us already run short of time. If you decide you're going to assume primary care giving responsibilities for Dad until he dies, what will you have to give up in order to be able to do that? Would you have to quit your job? Can you afford to do so? Could you benefit from the Family and Medical Leave Act?

Enacted in 1993, the Family and Medical Leave Act entitles most employees to take off 12 weeks within a 12-month period to care for a sick family member, a new baby, or to use as additional sick leave for themselves. The employee is not paid for the time missed, but her job must be available when she returns.

Another aspect of care giving you'll need to consider is physical strength and your own health. Are you physically strong enough to care for Dad? Are you really willing to be on call for 24 hours a day to meet his needs? As discussed in Chapter Eight, care giving is hard work, and you don't want to jeopardize your own health. Also, think about your own family. What do they think about your plans to care for Mom or Dad? Will you have to miss all of your children's school activities? Will your spouse feel neglected and resentful because you're spending so much time caring for a parent? As you can see, there are many considerations to think about when trying to decide the best way to care for your parent.

If you've thought it all over carefully, discussed the situation with your family, and decided that you're going to assume primary responsibility for Dad's care at the end of his life, know that you—and your family—are giving your father a great gift. You're showing him how much you love him, and showing him your appreciation for all the years he took care of you.

Caring For Your Parent at Home

You might decide to keep Mom at home for as long as possible and care for her there. Or, you may bring her to your own home. If possible, let her decide where she'd like to spend the end of her life. She may desperately want to die in the house where she's lived for years and years. Or, she might be more comfortable coming to your home, where there would be more people around and she could be close to you and your family. Either way, you'll want to make her as comfortable as possible.

Consider whether she may be more comfortable in a hospital bed than a family bed. This would allow you to adjust her position and make it easier for her to get out of bed, if she can. If it's difficult for her to get from one room to another, make the room in which she'll be spending most of her time as pleasant as possible. Place her bed near a window if you can, so that she can watch what's happening outside. You can always close the curtains if for some reason Mom doesn't want to see out. If she's able to move, or to be moved, ask her if she'd like to sit outside and feel the sunshine on her face and the breeze blowing. If she loves music, ask her if she'd like a CD player with some of her favorite tunes in her room. Give her all the choices that you can, and respect her dignity and her ability to decide what she wants or doesn't want.

It will help your parent tremendously to know that you and your family are fine, and will go on being fine without him. If you wail and moan and beg your father not to die because you can't get along without him, he's likely to feel burdened by your grief. He has no choice but to leave you. You don't want to increase the sorrow he's already feeling by adding guilt to it.

Make sure that her room and the bed linens are kept clean. If she can get up to use the bathroom, make sure there are grab bars on the sides of the toilet and no impediments between the bed and the bathroom. As discussed in Chapter Eight, if you'll be caring for Mom to the extent of helping her with a bedpan or changing bandages, you'll need to get some instructions from a home health agency or medical person. You'll need to learn how to keep Mom clean, and how to prevent her from getting bedsores.

Home health care personnel can teach you the practical aspects of caring for a loved one at home. They can teach you how Mom needs to be turned, how to make her bed, and wash her, and what to make for her to eat, and how to feed her if it comes to that. Home health care people can teach you many things, but they can't teach you what to say to your mother when she's awake at night and afraid of what's coming. They can't teach you how to tell her how much you love her, and they can't teach you how to tell her goodbye. These aspects of care giving must come from your heart.

Hospice Care

Although we're hearing more and more about the hospice concept of care in this country, many people still do not understand what it is. Hospice is not a place where people go to die, although there are places called hospices that offer specialized care for those who are approaching death. Hospice is a particular type of care for people who are dying.

The hospice concept can be traced back to medieval times, when special places were set up to provide comfort and shelter to travelers, religious people, and those who were dying, sick, or wounded. The word "hospice" comes from the Latin word "hospitium," which means guesthouse.

The modern hospice movement began in England during the 1960s when a doctor named Cicely Saunders set up St. Christopher's Hospice, just outside of London. St. Christopher's offered professional care giving with a team approach. It provided pain management techniques, but did not medically intervene to prolong the life of the dying patient. The hospice concept began to be noticed, and to spread. The first American hospice opened in 1974 in New Haven, Connecticut. There currently are about 3,100 hospice programs in the United States, treating more than half a million people a year. Most hospice care provided in the homes of those who are dying, or a home belonging to a family member. Some is provided in nursing home. Only 20 percent of hospice care occurs in a physical facility called a hospice.

The Hospice Foundation of America offers the following information about hospice care.

  • Hospice is a special concept of care designed to provide comfort and support to patients and their families when a life-limiting illness no longer responds to cure-oriented treatments.

- Hospice care neither prolongs life nor hastens death. Hospice staff and volunteers offer a specialized knowledge of medical care, including pain management.
- The goal of hospice care is to improve the quality of a patient's last days by offering comfort and dignity.
- Hospice care is provided by a team-oriented group of specially trained professionals, volunteers and family members.
- Hospice addresses all symptoms of a disease, with a special emphasis on controlling a patient's pain and discomfort.
- Hospice deals with the emotional, social and spiritual impact of the disease on the patient and the patient's family and friends.
- Hospice offers a variety of bereavement and counseling services to families before and after a patient's death.

If you are interested in learning more about hospice care and whether it may be the right approach for your parent, there is a lot of information available. Your parent's doctor or the hospital discharge planner should be able to give you information about hospice programs in your area. Check the yellow pages of your phone book under hospice, or contact your local area agency on aging, the Visiting Nurse Association, or the American Cancer Society. Many houses of worship can provide information about hospice care.

Hospice care is not for everyone. It puts family members in close contact with their loved one who is dying, and not everyone can handle that. It encourages family members to accompany their loved one on her journey toward death, and to help her make the passage from living to dying.

Hospice also takes a hands-off approach concerning medical intervention that will prolong the life of the dying person. In fact, a person must agree not to seek treatment intended to cure the illness in order to be a part of a hospice program. Hospice offers palliative care rather than curative care. Palliative care is intended only to relieve pain and control symptoms—not to cure the illness. Hospice care is available only to people whose doctors have certified their life expectancy of six months or less, although there is no penalty if the person lives longer. If the patient seems to be getting better during the course of hospice care, however, he certainly is free to discontinue the hospice program and return to the traditional medical system.

Hospice care is covered by Medicare, and by Medicaid in many states. If your parent is interested in enrolling in a hospice program, make sure you find one in your area that's Medicare certified. If Dad has a Medicare managed care plan, he still should be covered for hospice care.

- Some of the hospice-care benefits that Medicare covers include:
- Skilled nursing and therapy services
- Doctor's visits
- Volunteer services
- Nutritional counseling
- Spiritual counseling
- Short-term inpatient care in some instances
- Grief counseling for family members
- Medical social services
- Medical equipment necessary for the patient's care
- Most prescription drug costs
- Home care

Medicare offers a booklet called Medicare Hospice Benefits. You can get it from the office of any hospice program in your area, or through Medicare's web site at www.medicare.gov.

Hospice care is considered to be a holistic, loving form of care. Many people, however, are bothered by the fact that hospice care does not seek to cure. We tend to think our advanced medical system should be able to cure anything, and it's hard for many people to accept that a cure may not be possible. If you're interested in learning more about the hospice program, check the web sites listed below:

- Hospice Net at www.hospicenet.org
- Hospice Web at www.teleport.com/~hospice (includes a national hospice directory)
- Health Care Financing Administration at www.hcfa.gov/medicaid/ltc2.htm
- Hospice Cares at www.hospice-cares.com
- Hospice Foundation of America at www.hospicefoundation.org
- The National Hospice and Palliative Care Organization at www.nhpco.org

Honoring Your Parent's Wishes

Your parent may have strong wishes regarding the manner in which he dies, what treatments he receives, and what happens to his body after death. Sometimes, sadly enough, these wishes never get discussed because we find that type of conversation so difficult.

If you can't talk to Dad about his wishes concerning his dying, death and the disposal of his body, ask him to write them down so you can make sure they're recognized and followed. Different people wish for different things, and we can't be sure what someone wants until they tell us.

Maybe you're assuming Dad would like to die at home, when he really would prefer to be in a hospital so that he's not a burden to you and your family. Perhaps you think that Mom wants to be cremated because Dad was, when she actually prefers to be buried.

You can't honor your parent's wishes if you don't know what they are. Once you do know, assure your mother or father that you'll do everything in your power to make sure his or her wishes are carried through.

Planning a Funeral

Funerals are another topic of conversation we tend to avoid, particularly when the funeral relates to us, or someone we love. Unfortunately, we all will have to confront the funeral issue sooner or later.

Death is always a shock, no matter how sick a person had been before it. When death is sudden and unexpected, it is, on some levels, even more difficult to deal with. Sometimes, a survivor will be too distraught, or too much in shock to plan a funeral for a loved one. Often, however, planning a funeral or memorial service is extremely helpful. It gives family members a chance to work together on a task that expresses love and respect for the person who has died.

My father loved music, and his funeral was filled with it. Family members sang, read poetry, and expressed their thoughts and memories about him. Funerals always are sad occasions, but his had an underlying joy as we celebrated and honored the man he was and the live he lived.

Every funeral or memorial service is highly personal, and will reflect the personality of the deceased and his family and friends. When you need to plan a funeral, don't restrict it to what you've seen before, or what your minister or rabbi recommends. Think about what the person who has died loved, and what best reflects his personality. Let the funeral express those things.

Finding Out What You Can do Ahead of Time

A recent trend has been toward pre-planning funerals. Spouses often will do this together, and there are several benefits of pre-planning.

You can be assured that you'll get the type of funeral and burial that you want.

Your family members will know exactly what you want and won't have to make difficult decisions at the time of your death.

Pre-planning allows you to compare prices and services and get the best value possible. Families planning a funeral immediately following the death of a loved one often overspend because they're pressed to make quick, and often difficult, decisions.

Find out if your parents have pre-planned their funerals. If they have, make sure you know where the instructions are, and whether or not the funeral has been paid for in advance. Some people have funeral insurance, so ask about that possibility. Don't assume that if Dad dies suddenly, Mom will come forth with his funeral pre-plan and insurance certificate. Intense grief renders some people virtually helpless, and it's possible that Mom will have forgotten all about funeral plans that she and Dad completed five years ago.

If Dad has pre-planned his funeral, all you'll need to do is call the funeral home with which he's registered. Personnel there should do everything else, or will tell you exactly what you need to do. If there are no funeral plans, you'll have to select a funeral home. Check with Mom or another family about this, many families have used the same funeral home for years. Working with a funeral home that knows your family can make the process a lot easier.

What to do if Dad Didn't Pre-Plan

After you contact a funeral director, you'll need to decide how to dispose of Dad's body. Hopefully, you'll at least know Dad's wishes concerning this. Does he want to be buried or cremated? If he wants to be buried, do you know where? Is there a family plot somewhere? A cemetery associated with his church or synagogue? A mausoleum? If he's cremated, what does he wish to have done with the ashes? Maybe Dad preferred that his body, or at least some of his organs, be donated either to science or as replacement organs.

If you decide to have a funeral, you'll need to figure out where it will be. Dad's place of worship or the funeral home are the typical choices, but families sometimes prefer just a graveside service, or perhaps an outdoor memorial service at a later time. There is no right or wrong type of funeral or memorial service. Will you need pallbearers to carry the casket? If so, how many, and who will they be? Many families ask that contributions be given to a favorite charity or cause in memory of the deceased—often instead of sending flowers. If you wish to do that, you'll have to determine which charity or charities would be applicable.

The funeral director typically will call or deliver Dad's obituary to your local paper, but he'll need to get the information from you. This is very important, and something you should take some time to think about. If you forget to tell the funeral director that Dad graduated magna cum laude from Harvard in 1949, his obituary will not contain that information. Look over some obituaries from a few different newspapers, and note the type of information they include. Then write down everything you can think of that pertains to Dad's life and share it with the funeral director.

Most families have some sort of reception following a funeral. This can be at home, in a private room of a local restaurant, the church hall, an outside location, or anywhere that's convenient and available. Different families have different philosophies concerning these receptions. Some are solemn affairs, marking a very sad and difficult event, while others are more upbeat and party like. As with a funeral, there is no right or wrong type of reception. Just make sure that all family members are comfortable with what you decide to do.

Paying for a Funeral

Funerals can be expensive, there's no question about it. A typical funeral these days costs between $5,000 and $10,000, according to funeral plan.com, a web site that deals with many aspects of relating to death and funerals (find it at www.funeralplan.com).

If Dad's set aside money to pay for his funeral, and you know where it is and how to get to it, you at least won't have that worry. If he hasn't, there are several options to consider. Many people buy life insurance policies for the purpose of using them to pay for funeral expenses. Check and see if Dad has any policies earmarked for that purpose.

Another means of funding a funeral is through a funeral trust, which is when a funeral home opens a trust account in Dad's name. The trust, held at an area bank, is marked Pay On Death, and can be used only for funeral expenses. Make sure to look through all Dad's important papers so you can determine if he's made any sort of arrangements for funeral payment. If Dad was getting Medicaid or SSI, he may be eligible for some burial assistance. And, if he was a veteran, ask the funeral director to contact the Veteran's Administration to find out if he's eligible for any veteran's benefits.

If you're reading this chapter in advance of a parent's death, consider joining a memorial society. These are organizations that periodically compare funeral costs in their areas and pass the information along to their members. The idea is to help consumers plan funerals that are simple, dignified, and economical. There usually is a one-time charge for joining, usually $25 or $50. About half a million Americans now belong to memorial societies.

And, remember that funeral services, and their costs, vary greatly. According to the National Funeral Director's Association (NFDA), the cost of a casket can vary from $880 to $6,230, and other costs vary depending on location and the type of service you choose. You can get an idea of the costs of various services from the NFDA's web site at www.nfda.org.

Don't overspend on a funeral because you think you have to spend a lot of money to honor Dad, or to impress his friends (or yours), or to make up for something you didn't do for him while he was alive. Give him the nicest funeral that he, or you, can afford—planned with love and respect.

When Your Care Giving is Finished

Once Dad has died, your services as his caregiver will no longer be required. As you grieve for your loss, you may find yourself at loose ends, wondering what you should do, and actually missing the time you spent taking care of him. As difficult as care giving for Dad may have been, at least he was with you. You could talk to him, touch him, and tell him that you loved him. Now, he's gone.

Know that it's normal for you to feel empty and lost. There will be financial, legal, and practical matters you'll need to oversee. You may have to sort through Dad's clothes and other personal items and dispose of what's no longer wanted. You may have to clear out his house and put it up for sale. If Mom is still living, she'll no doubt need a great deal of help and support as she struggles to adjust to life without her spouse. You may have to serve as a go-between with her lawyer, accountant, or whoever else is involved in settling Dad's affairs or helping Mom with her legal and financial matters.

Maybe now that Dad is gone, Mom will need some help keeping up with her monthly bills or making decisions about the house. She may, after a time, consider moving. Mom also will need to grieve, and you'll have to let her do that in her own way, at her own pace. Take care of yourself during this time, even as you care for those around you who also are grieving. The time you spent taking care of your parent was stressful and difficult, and you need to take some time to rediscover your life as it was before you became Dad's caregiver. Spend time with your own family, and renew friendships that may have been neglected while you were busy taking care of Dad.

One last, and very important piece of advice is to be forgiving—both of yourself and of others. Taking care of an elderly parent, especially one who is sick—is extremely difficult. It's emotional, and it can be frustrating, wearisome, and trying. It's likely that from time to time while caring for Dad your patience ran short. You may have said some things—either to him or to another family member—which you now regret. You may have clashed with siblings or other family members about his care, their responsibilities, or financial matters. You might see now, in hindsight, that you could have helped Dad more if you'd done something differently or taken another course.

If any of those situations apply to you, do what you must to make amends. Apologize to those you may have hurt or offended. Chances are they're feeling bad about the same incident. If you feel that you let Dad down, or regret something you said to him before he died, tell him. Talk to him, or write him a letter and tell him exactly how you feel. When you're done, let those feelings go. Concentrate on all that you did to make the end of Dad's life more comfortable and pleasant than it might have been. Remember the moments you shared, and the closeness to him that you'll carry with you.

Once the worst of the grief and pain subsides, you'll remember better times with your parent. You'll understand that you helped as much as you could, and you'll realize what a gift you gave to him—when it was your turn.

Appendix: Resources

There are many resources available for caregivers. And, as greater attention turns to care giving and the needs of the elderly, we can expect to see even more. Some of those currently available are listed below.

Books
Berman, Claire Gallant. *Caring for Yourself While Caring for Aging Parents: How to Help, How to Survive.* Henry Holt & Company, Inc., 1997.

Carter, Rosalynn. *Helping Yourself Help Others.* Times Books, 1995.

Cohen, Donna and Eisdorfer, Carl. *Caring for Your Aging Parents: A Planning and Action Guide.* G. D. Putnam's Sons, 1993.

Hutchison, Joyce and Rupp, Joyce. *May I Walk You Home? Courage and Comfort for Caregivers of the Very Ill.* Ave Maria Press, 1999.

Johnson, Richard P., *Caring for Aging Parents: Straight Answers That Help You Serve Their Needs Without Ignoring Your Own.* Concordia Publishing House, 1997.

Kahana, Eva, et al. *Family Caregiving Across the Lifespan.* Sage Publications, 1994.

Karpinski, Marion. *The Home Care Companion's Quick Tips for Caregivers.* Healing Arts Communications, 2001.

Koch, Tom. *A Place in Time: Caregivers for Their Elderly.* Greenwood Publishing Group, 1993.

Kramer, Judy. *Changing Places: A Journey with My Parents Into Their Old Age.* The Putnum Publishing Group, 2000.

Lieberman, Trudy. *Complete Guide to Health Services for Seniors: What Your Family Needs to Know About Finding and Financing Medicare-Assisted Living Nursing Homes.* Crown Publishing Group, 2000.

Marcell, Jacqueline and Rodman, Shankle. *Elder Rage or, Take My Father . . . Please! How to Survive Caring for Aging Parents.* Impressive Press, 2001.

Morris, Virginia. *How to Care for Aging Parents.* Workman, 1996.

Murphy, Sylvia. *Dealing with a Death in the Family: How to Manage the Emotional and Practical Difficulties Surrounding a Death.* Trans-Atlantic Publications, Inc., 1997.

Rantz, Marilyn and Popejoy, Lori. *The New Nursing Homes: A 20-Minute Way to Find Great Long-Term Care*, Fairview Press, 2001.

Rhodes, Linda Colvin, Ed.D. *The Complete Idiot's Guide to Caring for Aging Parents.* Macmillan USA, Inc., 2001.

Scileppi, Kenneth P., *Caring for the Parents Who Cared for You: What to Do When an Aging Parent Needs You.* Carol Publishing Group, 1996.

Shaw, Eva. *What to Do When a Loved One Dies: A Practical and Compassionate Guide to Dealing with Death on Life's Terms.* Dickens Press, 1994.

Whybrow, Ruth. *Caring for Elderly Parents*, Crossroad Publishing Company, 1996.

Web Sites

Administration on Aging. Provides news, statistics, funding information, and information about the Older Americans Act. Located at www.aoa.dhhs.gov.

American Association of Homes and Services for the Aging. Addresses a variety of topics, including how to find an appropriate nursing home for your parent. Located at www.aahsa.org.

The American Association of Retired Persons. Provides information and offers resources on a great variety of issues affecting older people. Located at www.aarp.org.

Caregivers.com. Addresses many issues facing caregivers and provides links to other sites. Located as www.caregivers.com.

Children of Aging Parents. A comprehensive site including referrals and information, educational materials, a caregiver's guide, and bulletin boards. Located at www.caps4caregivers.org.

Christian Caregivers. Issues specific to those caring for chronically ill children or adults. Located at www.christiancaregivers.com.

Department of Veterans Affairs. Outlines benefits, facilities, and special programs for veterans. Located at www.va.gov.

ElderCare Online. Provides information, education, and support for caregivers. Located at www.ec-online.net.

ElderWeb. Offers a wide range of topics affecting older people and many links to other sites. Located at www.elderWeb.com.

Family Caregiver Alliance. An information resource on long-term care. Located at www.caregiver.org.

Health Answers. Provides information on general health, specific diseases and prescription drugs. Located at www.healthanswers.com.

Health Care Financing Administration. Federal agency that administers the Medicare and Medicaid health insurance programs. Located at www.hcfa.gov.

National Association of Area Agencies on Aging. Gives information about the Area Agencies on Aging, as well as general information about aging and links to local area agencies on aging. Located at www.n4a.org.

National Family Caregivers Association. Resources for caregivers on a variety of topics. Addresses the common needs and concerns of all family caregivers. Located at www.nfcacares.org.

National Institute of Health. Includes the Medline information service, consumer health information, and health information index. Located at www.nih.gov.

Partnership for Caring. Addresses end-of-life issues. Located at www.partnershipforcaring.org.

Social Security Online. Provides information about benefits, personal earnings, and benefit earning statement. Located at www.ssi.gov.

Index